VIOLENCE AND MENTAL ILLNESS

PSYCHOLOGY AND CRIME

General Editors: Brian Bornstein, University of Nebraska,
and Monica Miller, University of Nevada, Reno

Violence and Mental Illness

Rethinking Risk Factors and Enhancing Public Safety

Eric B. Elbogen *and* Nico Verykoukis

NEW YORK UNIVERSITY PRESS

New York

NEW YORK UNIVERSITY PRESS
New York
www.nyupress.org

Please contact the Library of Congress for Cataloging-in-Publication data.
ISBN: 9781479801442 (hardback)
ISBN: 9781479801459 (paperback)
ISBN: 9781479801473 (library ebook)
ISBN: 9781479801466 (consumer ebook)

This book is printed on acid-free paper, and its binding materials are chosen for strength and durability. We strive to use environmentally responsible suppliers and materials to the greatest extent possible in publishing our books.

Manufactured in the United States of America

10 9 8 7 6 5 4 3 2 1

Also available as an ebook

CONTENTS

Introduction

The Danger of Repeatedly Blaming Mental Illness for Violence

On January 15, 2022, a man took four members of a Texas synagogue hostage at gunpoint. The *New York Times* and the *New York Post* published nearly identical headlines within 48 hours: "Texas Synagogue Hostage Taker had 'Mental Health Issues,' Brother in U.K. Says"[1] and "Texas synagogue hostage-taker had 'mental health issues,' brother says,"[2] respectively, in their top news stories. Both media outlets made editorial decisions to prioritize attributing the violent act to the hostage taker's alleged mental health problems.

The information conveyed by these newspapers was not based on multiple reliable sources but solely on a single statement from the hostage taker's brother. The brother did not say, however, that the hostage taker had a history of mental health treatment. Nor did he relate that the hostage taker had a mental health diagnosis—there was no mention of depression, bipolar disorder, or schizophrenia. Instead, the brother used the phrase "mental health issues," which could apply to almost anyone reading this paragraph. The phrase "mental health issues" supplies an irrefutable excuse because every person has mental health issues at some point in their lives. But this phrase quickly morphed in the media. Reuters reported that the hostage taker "suffered from mental illness."[3] A substantial portion of the public was thus led to blame mental illness for this terroristic act.

In the following week, more information about the hostage taker emerged. He had a history of criminal and antisocial behavior dating back decades.[4] He was arrested in the 1990s and sent to a young offenders' institute when he was 19 years old. He was sentenced to six months in prison after using a baseball bat in a physical altercation with his cousins.[5] The hostage taker was banned from a court in England after angry outbursts in September 2001 in reaction to the New York City

9/11 attack.[6] He was reported to have a history of selling drugs and was extreme in his religious views and sexist behavior.[7] He was in prison three times between 1996 and 2012 for violent conduct, harassment, and theft.[8] In 2020, MI5, the British security service, investigated the hostage taker as a violent threat.[9] Months before he flew to the United States, some members of his family died, including his brother, who died from COVID complications.[6]

Within days of arriving in the United States, he had the resourcefulness to buy a semiautomatic pistol, despite not being a US citizen. He showed little unusual behavior in the days leading up to the hostage taking[10] and eluded notice in New York City and Dallas.[6] He did nothing to indicate any symptoms of a psychiatric disorder. Instead, he formulated an organized plan, mapping out precise steps to take members of a synagogue hostage at gunpoint. He aimed to negotiate the release of a Pakistani woman who was celebrated in Islamist militant circles and incarcerated in a nearby federal prison.[11]

This progression of news coverage is not atypical. When a mass shooting or violent incident worthy of national media coverage occurs, news outlets, politicians, pundits, and others often blame mental illness for the violence,[12] typically within 24 to 48 hours, often based on a vague statement by a family member, neighbor, or coworker. Mental health and forensic experts then follow this reaction to remind the public that mental illness does not cause most violence. Such discussion typically continues for a day or two. Sometimes mental illness is present in the offender, and sometimes it is not.

But mentioning mental illness at that early point is speculative nine times out of ten. Most facts are still unknown, and a mental health expert has not yet evaluated the offender. When (and if) the media reports other information, it is often days later, and their audience has likely moved on to other stories. The public largely remains in the dark about the other factors contributing to the violence. The media and public are caught in this cycle when violence occurs that has been deemed newsworthy.

When the public, politicians, or news media state that a perpetrator has "mental illness," they rarely mean that the perpetrator has social phobia, alcohol or opioid addiction, personality disorders, or Alzheimer's dementia, even though the diagnostic manual of the American

Psychiatric Association calls these all "mental disorders."[13] Instead, when most people use the term "mental illness," they are typically referring to psychotic disorders like schizophrenia, bipolar disorders (formerly called "manic depression"), or major depressive disorders, which the Substance Abuse and Mental Health Services Administration (SAMHSA) calls "serious mental illness."[14] Given that this book concerns how the public perceives mental illness and violence and reviews research on the link between these diagnoses and violence, we will use the term "mental illness" to refer to psychotic, bipolar, and major depressive disorders.

In light of this, several facts need to be considered. First, *mental illness is not necessary for violence to occur.* Only a fraction of violence (about 5%) perpetrated is attributable to psychotic, bipolar, or major depressive disorders.[15-18] In other words, the vast majority of violence is *not* directly connected to mental illness.

Second, *mental illness is not sufficient for violence to occur.* "Lacking empathy," "criminal thinking," and "hatred" are *not* symptoms of schizophrenia, bipolar disorder, or major depression. Every study on the subject shows that most people with mental illness are not violent. Indeed, people with these mental illnesses are more likely to be victims of violence than those without.[19-21]

Third, *mental illness and violence are related but the link is weaker than people think.* Mental illness is not a leading cause of violence in society though people with mental illness report higher violence rates than those without mental illness. How much "higher" depends on whether the person with mental illness has other risk factors, such as having a history of being physically abused, having a parent who was incarcerated, living in poverty, being unemployed and financially strained, or having inadequate social support. People with mental illness are more vulnerable to these risk factors than others. In this sense, it is simplistic to say mental illness is "the" cause of a violent act because this illness exists within a web of multiple risk factors. Mental illness doesn't exist in a vacuum; one cannot artificially isolate it from the rest of a person and say it is the single and only cause of a violent act.

Fourth, *mental illness and mental health issues are different.* In the United States, the lifetime prevalence of psychotic disorders, bipolar disorders, or major depressive disorders is approximately 20%.[22,23]

This prevalence rate translates to an estimated 51.6 million adults in the United States who will experience mental illness during their lives.[24] Further, mental illness is distinct from "mental health issues": nearly everyone at some point experiences sadness, anxiety, stress, worry, paranoia, or some other mental health symptom.

Recognizing this illustrates how easy it is to find that a perpetrator of violence has had "mental health issues" or showed "disordered thinking" and to then retrofit it as an after-the-fact explanation for the violence. Given its ubiquity, the term "mental health issues" can be used as a "reason" for violence perpetrated almost all the time. But as we can see in the example of the hostage taker, the problem is that the terms "mental illness" and "mental health issues" can be easily mixed up. This mix-up is not merely semantic but has real consequences by stigmatizing people with mental illness. Moreover, in a rush to explain violence, the news media, politicians, and the public frequently give little evidence to back up claims of mental illness. And many risk factors are uncovered only after the commencement of a criminal trial or through extensive forensic and law enforcement investigation—neither of which is likely to garner as much media attention as the original violence.

Rethinking Risk Factors to Prevent Violence

Think of each act of violence like a jigsaw puzzle made up of a number of different pieces. When violence occurs, people frequently think the puzzle is formed by one big piece: mental illness. "That's why the violence happened," people tell themselves. But at this point, this is usually just a guess. The reality is that mental illness is most often not a piece of the puzzle, and when it is, it is a small one. When present, mental illness often links with other puzzle pieces, such as alcohol abuse or poverty. The danger of exaggerating the role of mental illness is that it downplays the role of other important puzzle pieces, such as hate, anger, and past antisocial behavior. If we do not address all the pieces and their interplay, society will not solve the puzzle of violence.

The knee-jerk reaction of blaming mental illness in highly publicized violence diverts attention from more credible (if less sensational) puzzle pieces. For example, research shows that psychopathic and antisocial traits, substance abuse, being male, and younger age are among the strongest predictors of violence. By contrast, evidence shows that mental illness is a lesser factor in violent behavior.

Unless public dialogue takes multiple risk factors into account in the immediate aftermath of publicized violent acts, society will remain stuck in the same cycle of pointing fingers and pitting single causes of violence against other single causes. Policies to mitigate violence are more likely to stall, and improvements to public safety will likely fail. This book attempts to change course by pointing out the following:

(1) Blaming mental illness for well-publicized violent acts exaggerates the role of mental illness in violence. There is a long history of stigma against people with mental illness, perpetuated by news, media, and politicians, and maintained by cognitive biases. All interfere with an accurate appraisal of the multiple causes underlying each act of violence.

(2) No solid or consistent scientific evidence proves a strong link between mental illness and severe violence such as homicide.[21] Mental illness ranks low among risk factors for many different types of violent acts. Numerous other risk factors show stronger or more consistent links to violence, including being young and male, criminal background, gun access, anger dysregulation, psychopathic traits (including lacking empathy and remorse), alcohol and drug abuse, and poverty.

(3) Simplifying the conceptualization of violence by blaming mental illness will lead to suboptimal interventions to prevent violence because this shifts our focus away from paying attention to more vital risk factors. As a result, society misses opportunities to put policies and other safeguards in place that would protect us from a progression to violence.

Exaggerating the role of mental illness crowds out consideration of other risk factors with stronger links to violence, which, in turn, skews public policy on how best to prevent violence. Our central thesis is that expanding policies and interventions to prioritize stronger risk factors— thereby addressing a broader range of multiple risk factors—will lead to more effective societal approaches to preventing violence.

What is the origin of this exaggeration about mental illness and violence? How is it perpetuated? Why does the cycle continue to recur in which media pundits, politicians, and even ordinary citizens at once assume that a perpetrator must have mental illness and that this condition explains the violence? While other books address the prevalence of violence—with some arguing that violence has declined over time and is at its lowest rate in history[25]—the current book aims to better understand the perils of the general public instantly and frequently blaming mental illness for violence when it does happen. We offer an alternative way of thinking that focuses on a more comprehensive variety of risk factors for violence.

To achieve this goal, we first examine the definition of "mental illness," discuss its strengths, and describe alternative models. Medical tools like X-rays or MRIs that provide objective physical and biological data to diagnose medical disorders do not currently exist to diagnose mental disorders, which are primarily based on subjective reports of symptoms. One consequence is that this leaves the public vulnerable to misunderstanding mental illness and misusing its terminology. This lack of concision enables laypeople to loosely use the term "mental health issues" to explain acts they find otherwise unexplainable. When someone perpetrates horrific violence, observers often do not want to accept that a "rational" person could commit such an act, which opens the door to blaming mental illness.

Stigmatizing people with mental illness is a harmful act but not a new one. This social stigma separates people with mental illness from people without mental illness. But as previously discussed, we all have mental health issues at some point in our lives. Everyone has the potential to meet criteria for mental illness or mental disorder. So a separation of "them" (i.e., people with mental illness) from "us" (i.e., people without mental illness) is artificial and ultimately false. Separation perpetuates further unfounded fear about people with mental illness through the use of dehumanizing language and labels (e.g., the use of inflammatory descriptions like "mentally ill monsters"). We argue further that blaming mental illness for violence can be seen as scapegoating, picking as it does a vulnerable group to blame for misfortune—or, in this case, violence.

These powerful social forces are reinforced in the news and media. As a result, society perpetuates exaggeration about the link between mental illness and violence, as do individuals' cognitive biases. First, the "availability heuristic" shows that people think something is important because it is readily accessible to memory. Given that the news, media, and politicians regularly offer mental illness as the explanation for a violent act, this risk factor comes to mind quickly and, therefore, is inaccurately perceived as more critical for violence than it is.

Second, the "fundamental attribution error" suggests that people discount environment-level variables and overemphasize individual-level variables when evaluating other people's behavior. This means that the individual-level variable of mental illness is more likely to be blamed for violence than environmental-level risk factors such as being a member of an online hate group, inadequate family and social support, childhood physical abuse, financial strain, or having access to guns and semi-automatic assault rifles.

Third, the "theater of control" means people prefer explanations that confer an ability to control a solution. Many in the public believe (or want to believe) that mental health professionals can accurately predict violence, effectively treat and prevent violence, and know when a patient is planning violence, even though mental health professionals are limited in each. The mental health field can and does help as best as it can; but given these limitations in the field and given that mental illness is a weaker factor in violence than generally perceived, mental health professionals can only go so far.

If social stigma and cognitive biases contribute to a distorted view of the link between mental illness and violence, then this begs the question: what is a more informed view? We review current scientific studies on the link between mental illness and violence, highlighting their strengths and limitations. We also investigate the strength of violence risk factors and how mental illness compares to other risk factors for multiple types of violence: domestic violence, targeted school violence, sex offenses, intimate partner homicide, stalking, child sexual abuse, attacks against government officials, campus violence, and mass attacks.

This overview reveals that neither mental illness nor mental health problems were ranked among the top five risk factors for *any* type of violence examined. When listed, mental health problems were among the lowest ranked risk factors for violent acts. Other risk factors show much stronger correlations with violence.

By analyzing risk factors for these multiple types of violence, we argue that violence risk factors fall into three distinct categories. Applying the jigsaw puzzle metaphor, we discover that violence risk factors can be placed into three piles:

(1) External risk factors (environment-level variables such as poverty, financial strain, inadequate social support)
(2) Internal risk factors (individual-level variables such as younger age, difficulty managing anger, co-occurring substance abuse and mental illness)
(3) Violence-defining risk factors that make a violent action a more viable and acceptable option for a person (e.g., antisocial personality traits, gun access, hate group/gang membership)

The more risk factors in all three categories, the higher the odds of violence. Categories 1 and 2 increase a person's risk of violence statistically but are, by definition, not necessarily related to violence. A person can live under financial strain or abuse alcohol, and these factors certainly elevate the chances of a person becoming violent. But in and of themselves, these risk factors are not necessary for violent behavior to occur: though they increase the risk of violence, living under financial strain or abusing alcohol are not required components for violent acts.

Instead, the risk factors in the third category increase a person's risk of violence statistically *and* are related to the very act of violence itself: a person will commit a violent act when they believe it is acceptable to be violent and have the means to complete that violent act. Extending the example in the previous paragraph, a person poses an extremely high risk of perpetrating violence if they are under financial strain, abuse alcohol, have anger that transforms into hatred inspired by online groups, can access an arsenal of weapons, feel no empathy toward others, and express no qualms at the prospect of killing people.

At its essence, every violent act involves a person who, in the moment, has access to the means to harm others and feels they have the "green light" to be violent. Therefore, a risk factor under the third category would be the belief that it is neither improper nor wrong to harm others (i.e., "violence is okay"). Another related risk factor in this category would be a person assigning little to no weight to others' pain and suffering—even the pain of those closest to them. Violence-defining risk factors are like the puzzle pieces with straight edges that are usually piled up first so that the frame of the jigsaw puzzle can be defined.

These considerations are often missed by the public and media. For a person to reach such a state as to commit violence, there are factors that increase the chances that person will be violent as well as factors that additionally define the very act of violence itself. As such, we argue that society must change the narrative about violence: rather than falling back on unfounded exaggerations about mental illness and violence, there is a need to think more clearly about the many factors involved in perpetrating violent acts, especially stronger risk factors and those that both increase violence risk and define violent acts.

Using a range of empirical data, we aim to change the first question asked in the face of violence from "Did mental illness cause this violence?" (i.e., extremely narrow focus on a singular cause of violence) to a second question we should ask: "What are the other stronger causes of this violence we need to consider?" (i.e., broader focus on multiple causes of violence). What are the puzzle pieces we need to explain this act of violence? In illuminating the link between violence and these three categories of risk factors, we seek to advance more effective interventions and policies to enhance public safety and prevent violent acts in the future.

1

Current Definitions and Understanding
of Mental Illness

Nestled in a leafy campus in Bethesda, Maryland, is the National Institute of Mental Health (NIMH), the United States' lead federal agency for
research on mental illness. On its website, NIMH writes:

> Serious mental illness (SMI) is defined as a mental, behavioral, or emo-
> tional disorder resulting in serious functional impairment, which sub-
> stantially interferes with or limits one or more major life activities. The
> burden of mental illnesses is particularly concentrated among those who
> experience disability due to SMI.[26]

SMI interferes with effective personal and occupational functioning,
distorts the experience of reality (delusions, hallucinations), and dimin-
ishes a person's judgment and autonomy. According to the Substance
Abuse and Mental Health Services Administration (SAMHSA), SMI
includes (1) schizophrenia and other psychotic disorders, (2) bipolar
disorders, and (3) major depressive disorders.[14] These three sets of disorders are associated with dramatic disruptions of thought, mood, and
behavior. An estimated 20% of American adults have a lifetime history
of SMI, 5% currently meeting criteria according to the NIMH.[26]

These diagnoses are also called SMI by advocacy groups, for example,
the National Alliance for the Mentally Ill (NAMI). Many people who
receive publicly funded Social Security Disability Income (SSDI) due
to psychiatric disability have one of these three SMI diagnoses. The
chronic course of SMI has debilitating effects on an individual's quality
of life. Their powerful impact on daily functioning makes people with
SMI convenient, but mistaken, candidates for singular blame in acts of
violence, especially newsworthy violence.

The *Diagnostic and Statistical Manual of Mental Disorders* (DSM) published by the American Psychiatric Association uses a different term,

"mental disorder," to denote a wider range of *all* psychiatric conditions, not just the three diagnoses that constitute SMI.[13] Distinguishing SMI from the much larger domain of mental disorders requires a closer look at the DSM.

At nearly 1000 pages containing hundreds of disorders and thousands of symptoms, the DSM is as dense as it is heavy. Like any manual, whether for a household refrigerator or the rules of Major League Baseball, it is detailed, formal, and dry. Though a target of criticism owing to the subjective qualities inherent in developing and applying psychiatric diagnoses, the DSM is nonetheless an impressive accomplishment and the only manual that exclusively defines and sets standard criteria for mental disorders.

Before the first DSM was published in 1952, American psychiatric care was varied and disjointed. In addition to helping maintain robustness, the DSM was the beginning of a common language psychiatrists could use to communicate about their work, no matter where they practiced (inpatient, outpatient, private hospital, state institution, etc.) or where they had trained (psychoanalytic institute, military hospital, research university, etc.).

In 2022, the American Psychiatric Association published the *Diagnostic and Statistical Manual of Mental Disorders-Fifth Edition-Text Revision* (DSM-5-TR). The DSM-5 classifies a vast number of mental disorders, well over 100, and covers a range of milder to more severe diagnoses.[13] On one end of this continuum, a person may suffer from chronic, mild-to-moderate anxiety (excessive worry, periodic shortness of breath, feelings of panic). This may cause distress but not dysfunction. On the other end of the continuum, a person may suffer from major depression with psychotic features such as hearing voices to harm oneself. This would substantially interfere with daily functioning.

DSM-5 "mental disorders" are categorized according to the following domains: Neurodevelopmental Disorders (e.g., autism, intellectual disorder), Psychotic Disorders (e.g., schizophrenia), Bipolar Disorders, Depressive Disorders, Anxiety Disorders (e.g., phobias, panic attacks), Obsessive-Compulsive Disorders, Trauma- and Stressor-Related Disorders (e.g., posttraumatic stress disorder, or PTSD), Dissociative Disorders, Somatic symptoms and related disorders, Feeding and Eating Disorders, Elimination Disorders, Sleep-Wake Disorders, Sexual Dysfunction, Gender Dysphoria, Disruptive, Impulse-Control, and

Conduct Disorders (e.g., intermittent explosive disorder, antisocial personality disorder), Substance-Related and Addictive Disorders (e.g., Alcohol-Related, Opioid-Related), Neurocognitive Disorders (e.g., dementia), Personality Disorders (e.g., borderline, antisocial), and Paraphilic Disorders (e.g., pedophilia).

So, the category "serious mental illness" (SMI) encompasses three DSM-5 domains of mental disorders. First, schizophrenia and other psychotic disorders, which include the following key symptoms: delusions (fixed beliefs not rooted or only loosely rooted in reality), hallucinations (perceptual distortions such as hearing or seeing things that are not there), disorganized thought and speech, abnormal behavior like agitation or rigid posturing, and so-called negative symptoms like diminished expression and decreased motivation.[13] The lifetime prevalence of schizophrenia is 0.7% according to the DSM-5.[13]

The second, "bipolar disorder," which was formerly called "manic-depressive disorder," includes the symptoms of major depression, periodically alternating with symptoms of mania or hypomania including decreased need for sleep, increased talkativeness, grandiosity, racing thoughts, and excessive engagement in activities like impulsive shopping sprees, risky sexual behaviors, or foolish financial decisions.[13] The lifetime prevalence is 4.4% according to the NIMH.[26]

The third, major depressive disorder includes sad mood, reduced interest or pleasure in activities, significant weight change (gain or loss), insomnia, agitation, fatigue, feelings of worthlessness or guilt, diminished attention and concentration, and suicidal ideation.[13] The lifetime prevalence rate is 20.6% according to epidemiological research.[27]

As mentioned earlier, because this book concerns how the public perceives mental illness and violence as well as summarizes research on the link between violence and these three diagnoses, we will use the term "mental illness" to refer to psychotic, bipolar, and major depressive disorders and to be synonymous with SMI. The following case vignettes will help illustrate these three mental illnesses.

Schizophrenia

David was a 35-year-old man raised in an intact family, some of whom had histories of bipolar disorder and depression. There was a possible history of David witnessing violence between his parents, but he would refuse to talk about it when asked about his childhood. He got Bs and Cs in high school; after graduation he trained to become a heating-ventilation-air-conditioning (HVAC) technician, which he excelled at for many years. David married a loving and supportive wife who worked as a registered nurse, and the couple had two sons and a daughter.

About 12 years after graduating high school, David began experiencing paranoia (fears that people wanted to break into his home and hurt him and his family) and auditory hallucinations (voices telling him that he was a loser and worthless). Shortly thereafter, he attempted suicide by overdosing on pain medication. But he survived, and after inpatient psychiatric treatment, his condition improved. He was diagnosed with paranoid schizophrenia. Because he failed to maintain outpatient treatment posthospitalization, he returned to inpatient treatment at his wife's insistence.

After making significant improvement during his second hospital stay, David stuck to his plan of monthly psychiatrist appointments, daily and then weekly meetings with his case manager, and psychosocial support through the local mental health center, including vocational counseling and regular socializing with other people coping with mental illness. Eventually, he returned to work full-time as an HVAC technician. He reduced his treatment to monthly psychiatric appointments and biweekly check-ins with his case manager.

Like many people experiencing mental illness, David had many strengths. While in treatment and stable, he was warm, optimistic, and had a great sense of humor. He was a good husband, father, and co-worker. His wife and family were functional and supportive. He was not violent toward anyone. He lived in a community with comprehensive mental health services available to all. He was an honest, cooperative, and active participant in his treatment. David's case shows how family, clinical, and community support can help someone with mental illness achieve optimal functioning.

Major Depression

Sarah was a 52-year-old woman who had suffered from major depression since her early 20s. She grew up in an intact family with a history of depression. Despite her chronic struggles with depressed mood, low energy, and negative thoughts, she managed to maintain a career as a manager at a large accounting firm and raise two children primarily by herself after she divorced her husband while in her 30s.

Sarah had a long outpatient treatment history of medication, monthly visits with her psychiatrist, regular involvement with a social support program for patients with mental illness, and check-ins with her counselor. She managed her more extreme lows with sick leave from work, and she was fortunate to have an employer who was supportive of her situation. Her proactive and consistent outpatient treatment and excellent communication with her employer allowed her to avoid hospitalization. Sarah's cooperative approach to her treatment and her lack of complicating factors like addiction, personality disorder, or severe medical issues allowed her to thrive with treatment and support. She never needed to be hospitalized.

Bipolar Disorder

Bryce was a 43-year-old man diagnosed with bipolar disorder in his 20s. He grew up in a family that faced constant financial stress. Bryce had experienced several concussions during a few fights at school, largely the result of being bullied by peers. During his 30s, he had several episodes indicative of bipolar disorder, including impulsive spending, staying awake for days at a time, and racing thoughts that were also disorganized and tangential. Although he had worked construction and odd jobs in early adulthood, by his 40s, Bryce was on Social Security disability and Medicare/Medicaid as a result of chronic mania, depression, and neuropsychological deficits.

A mix of inpatient, outpatient, and community support helped Bryce experience periods of stability interrupted by annual episodes of acute mental illness. Those episodes included impulsive spending (e.g., becoming delinquent on his multiple credit cards), wrecked vehicles, and eviction. Bryce required medicine, social support, housing support, and psychotherapy.

Yet Bryce, when relatively stable, was engaging, generous, upbeat, and fun to be around. He was, over time, treatment adherent and honest about his thoughts and feelings and learned to seek help if he started experiencing symptoms of mania. Although Bryce could be hotheaded and impulsive, he was not a bully. And he was fortunate to live in a locality with well-funded, comprehensive mental health services and eventually obtained a long-term job in a warehouse tracking inventory, enabling him to achieve stability in his life for decades.

Substance Dependence, Antisocial Personality Disorder, and Violence

In terms of social stigma generally and stigma as prone to violence specifically, people with mental illness tend to endure the worst, which we will discuss in the next chapter. Conversely, there are two mental disorders in the DSM-5 that one might surmise are more directly related to violence: (1) substance-related and addictive disorders and (2) antisocial personality disorder.

Substance-related and addictive disorders are the DSM-5 terms for what most people would recognize as alcohol and drug abuse or dependence. According to recent epidemiological data, approximately 29.1% have lifetime alcohol use disorder, and 9.9% have lifetime drug use disorder.[28] The DSM-5 provides general definitions applicable to everything from alcohol to cannabis to opiates: "The essential feature of a substance use disorder is a cluster of cognitive, behavioral, and physiological symptoms indicating that the individual continues using the substance despite significant substance-related problems."[13(p 483)]

While substance-related and addictive disorders can, much like mental illness, lead to dysfunction and debilitation, they are more behavior-based than symptom-based. With formal treatment or informal support groups like Alcoholics Anonymous and Narcotics Anonymous, many with these disorders can eventually stop using alcohol or drugs and no longer experience the mind-altering and physically debilitating effects of both using substances and withdrawing from them. But relative to mental illness, alcohol use disorder is a stronger candidate for blame in acts of violence. According to the DSM-5:

> Alcohol use disorder is associated with a significant increase in the risk of accidents, violence, and suicide. It is estimated that one in five intensive care unit admissions in some urban hospitals is related to alcohol and

that 40% of individuals in the United States experience an alcohol-related event at some point in their lives, with alcohol accounting for up to 55% of fatal driving events. Severe alcohol use disorder, especially in individuals with antisocial personality disorder, is associated with the commission of criminal acts, including homicide.[13(p 496)]

Criteria for alcohol use disorder, "a problematic pattern of alcohol use leading to clinically significant impairment or distress,"[13(p 490)] include consuming increasing amounts of alcohol, unsuccessful attempts to decrease consumption, increased cravings, increased tolerance, occupational and interpersonal problems, repeatedly experiencing physically hazardous situations (fistfights, car accidents, domestic violence, etc.), and physical withdrawal requiring medical care (inpatient or outpatient detoxification).

In a massive scientific literature review called a "meta-analysis"—a study that combines statistical information from published studies on a specific subject—researchers examined over 28,000 homicide offenders across nine countries and found that 48% of homicide offenders were under the influence of alcohol at the time of the offense, and 37% were intoxicated.[29]

Antisocial personality disorder is a personality type with specific problematic traits, which according to the DSM includes "a pervasive pattern of disregard for and violation of the rights of others, occurring since age 15 years"[13(p 659)] in addition to repeatedly performing criminal acts, deceitfulness, impulsivity, irritability and aggressiveness, disregard for the safety of self or others, consistent irresponsibility, and lack of remorse for harming others or breaking laws.[13] Also, the patient must be age 18 or older and have evidence of conduct disorder (a childhood version of antisocial personality disorder) before age 15.

Antisocial personality disorder overlaps with psychopathy, a psychological construct that covers intrapersonal traits (e.g., lacking empathy, lacking remorse, blaming others, grandiosity, manipulativeness, not taking responsibility) and interpersonal traits (e.g., antisocial behaviors, anger, impulsivity, poor coping strategies, deviant actions) and is strongly linked to acts of violence against others.[30] Correspondingly, people with antisocial personality disorder lack remorse for harming others and lack the quality that reliably prevents most people from harming others in the first place: empathy.[13(p660)] They believe, unlike most people, that crime and violence are acceptable methods for solving their problems and advancing their interests. They do not necessarily see other people like themselves, being valued and respected as they would like to be. Instead, they often see other people as a means to an end, as instruments to be used and discarded. People with antisocial personality disorder frequently view violence against others, both intimates and strangers, as necessary, desirable, and just.

The DSM-5's discussion of the prevalence rates of antisocial personality disorder highlights the dangerous intersection of males inclined toward violence and alcohol use disorder:

> Twelve-month prevalence rates for antisocial personality disorder, using criteria from previous DSMs, are between 0.2% and 3.3%. The highest prevalence of antisocial personality disorder (greater than 70%) is among most severe samples of males with alcohol use disorder and from substance abuse clinics, prisons, and other forensic settings. Prevalence is higher in samples affected by adverse socioeconomic (i.e., poverty) or sociocultural (i.e., migration) factors.[13(p 661)]

Studies find a lifetime prevalence of 3.3% for antisocial personality disorder.[31] Various combinations of personal entitlement, impulsivity, lack of remorse, lack of empathy, and interpersonal exploitation over time build the fuse for violence, as do other factors like substance abuse, financial stress, legal troubles, or marital conflict. The following vignette illustrates the complex interplay of mental illness, substance abuse, and antisocial personality disorder.

Depression, Alcohol Abuse, and Antisocial Personality Disorder

John was a 27-year-old man who had experienced depression starting in his teenage years, including periods in which he was irritable and sad, experienced erratic sleep patterns, and found it difficult to concentrate. His mother raised him after his parents divorced when he was young. He never had a relationship with his father, who had a heavy drinking history. Although John had academic difficulties (obtaining mostly grades of Cs and Ds) and got into fights in high school, he graduated and obtained an entry-level job in construction. He was prescribed antidepressant medication by his primary care physician.

Interpersonally, he had a history of conflicts with his ex-girlfriend who was the mother of his five-year-old daughter and two-year-old son. After an episode in which police responded to a domestic disturbance involving John shouting angrily at his ex-girlfriend on her front lawn, the Department of Social Services (DSS) was called and a social worker was required to chaperone his visits with his children.

John entered counseling intending to acquire unsupervised visits with his children. The therapist met with him every other week for four months. John presented as cooperative and pleasant, showed insight into past behavior, and reported more positive behavioral patterns. Treatment focused on coping skills for depression, anger management, and parenting skills. That said, John did not reveal to anyone that he increasingly managed his irritability and difficulty with sleep by self-medicating with alcohol, drinking after work and before bed each night. At one point, he was spending over $400 a month on beer and liquor, was falling behind on his rent, and risked eviction from his apartment. Nevertheless, in therapy, John reported fewer depressive symptoms. Based on their sessions, John's therapist believed that he was safe to have unsupervised visits with his children.

When John's case came before family court, evidence was submitted that in the past, John had been more violent and intimidating than he had led others to believe, including when he was drunk. On one occasion, he threatened to shoot the mother of his children and her parents with his firearm. This was documented in a police report. Based on this, the court ruled that unsupervised visits would not be allowed at that time. John was angry at the result, and after the hearing, he showed no remorse for having deceived others, including the therapist, about his alcohol abuse and violence. Instead, he blamed the criminal legal system, law enforcement, the judge, DSS, and his ex-girlfriend—but not himself—for losing parental rights.

John's case demonstrates that the combination of depression, alcohol misuse, and antisocial personality disorder can be associated with increased risk of violence. In cases like John's, the criminal legal system provides the ultimate gathering and filtering of facts to protect people at risk, especially minors. John's case also illustrates the limits of what clinicians can know about a client, especially when it is a client like John, whose antisocial traits (lying about intimidation and violence, lack of remorse) make for a shaky therapeutic alliance. This is an important point: even if mental illness comprises part of an individual's violence risk, mental health professionals have limitations in preventing violence.

Though John shared some mental health symptoms with David, Sarah, and Bryce, he did not experience them with the same debilitating force. While David, Sarah, and Bryce may have, at times like most people, experienced interpersonal conflicts, they did not exercise patterns of intimidation and abuse against someone or engage in patterns of lying and deceit. Unlike John, they understood and accepted that harming others is wrong and should be followed by remorse, apology, and improved behavior. Also, unlike John, they engaged in treatment to understand and address their issues, not to manipulate and control others. Those psychological and moral differences are why antisocial traits increase violence risk.

Blaming mental illness for John's risk of violence unfairly reinforces stigma and fear of mental illness, makes no one safer, and discounts stronger risk factors for violence (i.e., alcohol abuse, antisocial personality disorder). As shown in the descriptions of diagnoses and in these case studies, "lacking empathy," "criminal thinking," and "hatred" are *not* symptoms of schizophrenia, bipolar disorder, or major depression. Another crucial point is: though the DSM-5 classifies all psychiatric conditions as mental disorders, there are significant conceptual and practical distinctions between mental disorders and mental illnesses. Substance abuse and personality disorders are different from mental illness. Below, Table 1.1 summarizes differences in terminology between mental disorders, mental illness, and mental health symptoms/behaviors.

Defining Mental Disorders and Social Environment

Although the DSM represents the prevailing model of psychiatric diagnosis, it does have limitations. First, diagnosing mental disorders is based primarily on interviewing a patient, which relies on self-report and presumed honesty and accuracy in conveying one's symptoms. Psychiatrist Thomas Insel, who led NIMH from 2002 to 2015 before leaving

TABLE 1.1: Differentiating Mental Disorder, Mental Illness, and Mental
Health Symptoms/Behaviors

Mental Disorder	Mental Illness	Mental Health Symptoms/Behaviors	Lifetime Prevalence
Schizophrenia	Yes	Delusions, disorganized thoughts, hallucinations, catatonia, anhedonia	0.3%–0.7%
Bipolar disorder	Yes	Racing thoughts, impulsivity, extreme mood swings with highs (mania) and lows (depression)	4.4%
Major depressive Disorder	Yes	Sadness, loss of interest, change in sleep and appetite, suicidal thoughts	8.4%
Alcohol-related disorder	No	Alcohol addiction	29.1%
Other substance-related disorders	No	Stimulant, hallucinogen, inhalant, cannabis, opioid, and other drug addictions	9.9%
Antisocial personality disorder	No	Disregard for rights and safety of others, deceitfulness, hostile, impulsivity, irresponsibility, lack remorse for harming others or breaking laws	3.3%

for Mindstrong, Google's psychiatric division, discusses the problems
that result:

> The goal of this new manual, as with all previous editions, is to provide a
> common language for describing psychopathology. While DSM has been
> described as a "Bible" for the field, it is, at best, a dictionary, creating a
> set of labels and defining each. The strength of each of the editions of
> DSM has been "reliability"—each edition has ensured that clinicians use
> the same terms in the same ways. The weakness is its lack of validity.
> Unlike our definitions of ischemic heart disease, lymphoma, or AIDS,
> the DSM diagnoses are based on a consensus about clusters of clinical
> symptoms, not any objective laboratory measure. In the rest of medicine,
> this would be equivalent to creating diagnostic systems based on chest
> pain or the quality of fever. Indeed, symptom-based diagnosis, once com-
> mon in other areas of medicine, has been largely replaced in the past half
> century as we have understood that symptoms alone rarely indicate the
> best choice of treatment.[32]

In other words, because DSM diagnoses of mental disorders are based
largely on the subjective reports of symptoms, they lack the scientific

validity conferred by medical tools like X-rays or MRIs that provide objective physical and biological data to diagnose medical disorders.

Second, with more than 100 diagnoses, the DSM-5 represents an expansion of diagnoses and potentially associated pharmacological treatment into many areas of thought, mood, and behavior that are, arguably, simply part of life (e.g., feeling sad or stressed out). DSM-IV Task Force Chair Allen Frances in his 2014 book *Saving Normal* criticizes the DSM as "adding new diagnoses that would turn everyday anxiety, eccentricity, forgetting, and bad eating habits into mental disorders. . . . psychiatry expanded its boundaries to include many who are better considered normal."[33(pXV-XVI)] According to Frances, this expansion of diagnoses has enabled the labeling and medicalization of a set of behaviors that are not necessarily "disordered."

Third, DSM diagnoses focus on an individual's psychiatric symptoms given its intent to resemble a medical model approach to diagnosis that focuses on biological variables underlying medical conditions. But this comes at a cost because the DSM does not offer extensive evaluation of an individual's social environment. The DSM used to include a social and occupational functioning scale called the Global Assessment of Functioning (GAF) that was scored on a scale from 0 to 100. However, GAF, along with a diagnostic section noting a person's psychosocial and environmental problems, was removed from the DSM-5.

Nevertheless, other conceptualizations of mental illness exist that do emphasize a person's social environment. One such framework is what has been called "the biopsychosocial model," in which clinicians consider the biological, psychological, and social components of a patient's illness.[34,35] The biological part involves brain functioning, personal medical history, substance abuse effects, family history, and other physical ailments or injuries that could disrupt one's ability to function. The social part includes the patient's everyday environment and the people, places, and events that may create obstacles or even trauma in their lives. The psychological part includes habits of thought, emotion, and action.

The approach helps clinicians tailor treatment not only to diagnosis but also to each patient's situation. A patient with schizophrenia who lives with their parents and wants to reenter the workforce would benefit from medication management with their psychiatrist, vocational counseling with an occupational therapist, a family support group for transitional stress, and a case manager to coordinate the entire process. A patient with a history of alcohol abuse who receives a cancer diagnosis would benefit from oncology treatment, individual psychotherapy, regular Alcoholics Anonymous meetings, and a support group of fellow cancer patients. In this individualized way, the biopsychosocial approach (coordinated by a case manager, usually a nurse or a social worker who facilitates communication among treatment providers) best serves and validates the patient as a whole person with unique requirements.

This biopsychosocial model is consistent with the landmark report by the World Health Organization (WHO) calling for more attention to social determinants of health,[36] which "include the conditions in which people are born, live, work, and age, and the health systems they can access, which are in turn shaped by a wider set of forces: economics, social, environmental policies, and politics."[37(p392)] There is an overwhelming amount of evidence demonstrating clear links between social determinants and health outcomes.[38] Authors have applied this model of social determinants for understanding mental illness,[37] arguing that people living in poverty and those who live in socially disadvantaged neighborhoods are disproportionately more likely to have mental illnesses. Unemployment and lower educational attainment are also associated with mental illness.

Of note, the causal roles involved in the framework are bidirectional: unemployment can cause a person to become more depressed, and a person who is depressed may have more trouble keeping a job. It is most likely the two factors mutually reinforce one another. As such, an individual's mental health cannot be artificially isolated from their social environment: the two are inextricably connected and copresent. Thus, as suggested by the biopsychosocial model, a person's situation must be factored into understanding a person's mental illness. This distinction between a primary focus on psychiatric symptoms (as in the DSM) and a primary focus on interaction with one's social environment (as in the biopsychosocial model) will be critical to understanding how society thinks about violence and mental illness and then expanding the types of interventions society uses to prevent violence. In particular, environment-level factors need to be considered when understanding the many causes of violence and when developing a comprehensive array of strategies to prevent violence.

For the time being, the biopsychosocial model provides an important alternative to the DSM. Like any model, the biopsychosocial model is not without critics, who tend to argue that it is too general, too vague, and does not offer specific guidance for clinicians. Certainly, the model is more immediately applicable in specialties like primary care and outpatient psychiatry, where there is often more time to develop a treatment plan for chronic ailments, than in specialties like trauma surgery or neurosurgery, where an urgent and specific lifesaving medical procedure must be performed. Keep in mind, though, that the postoperative treatment plans of the latter patients, if they survive surgery, would address biopsychosocial needs such as medicine, wound care, physical therapy, occupational therapy, and speech therapy.

But what might happen if scientific research discovers definitive biological causes for mental illness or other mental disorders? In his book *The Disordered Mind*, Nobel Prize–winning psychiatrist and neuroscientist Eric Kandel of Columbia University describes the scientific progress that has been made over the past century regarding the biological basis of schizophrenia, bipolar disorder, and major depression, together the most challenging mental illnesses.[39] He explains in plain language how genetic research, brain imaging, and animal experiments continue to accumulate evidence, albeit not yet conclusive, of the physical roots of mental illness. Nevertheless, Dr. Kandel reminds that one must consider the interaction between genetic and social environmental factors in diagnosis and treatment of mental illness, as well as for understanding violent and aggressive behavior.[40]

In sum, the model of mental illness defined in the DSM is defined primarily by individual-level symptoms. Although the DSM-5 has limitations, creating diagnostic categories sharing similar qualities can lead to progress in research and practice, including identifying biological markers to establish scientific validity. It remains a valuable tool committed to self-reflection and self-improvement, which most clinicians properly use as a guide more than a mandate.

Alternative models such as the biopsychosocial model stress the role of social factors when thinking about an individual's mental health and the types of interventions that can be beneficial. This distinction between individual-level and environment-level factors and interventions foreshadows empirical research on the link between mental illness and violence and interventions to prevent violence that address both levels of variables.

As such, to understand the reasons behind a violent act, it will be essential that environment- and individual-level risk factors both need to be considered. Ensuring that violence is conceptualized according to multiple domains of risk factors enables expansion of the types of interventions that might also prevent violence. Before we discuss the science of violence risk factors and the strategies to curb violence, it is important to ask: why is the link between mental illness and violence exaggerated?

2

Social Stigma and Exaggerations about
Mental Illness and Violence

Encountering an actively psychotic person—for example, a person on the street experiencing homelessness talking angrily to themselves— can be as disconcerting for a trained mental health professional as for a layperson. Psychosis disrupts the sufferer's ability to function effectively in public and signal to others that they are safe and predictable citizens. Even trained, aware, compassionate people can have a tough time responding to a person who is disheveled, soiled, shouting, urinating, or otherwise behaving erratically and bizarrely in a public space. Should one try to help? Pretend the person with mental illness is not there? Cross the street?

Deeply held convictions to be respectful of all human beings may falter. Such public encounters can increase hunger for social control, albeit in jails (if hospital beds are too few or too costly), and decrease patience for social and psychological understanding. And unless people already have an experience from their own struggles, or from growing close to someone with a mental illness through some facet of their personal or work life, all they may know of psychiatric patients may be those troubling public encounters. As a result, few have the opportunity to see the positive results, often dramatic, of sustained medicine, psychotherapy, and social support, which help the symptoms recede and the person's humanity emerge.

When encountering the actively psychotic person, the public also rarely gets to reflect on the thousands of other people with mental illness they have perhaps stood by or walked right next to but whose mental illness was invisible because they were not symptomatic to such an extreme degree (like David, Sarah, and Bryce from the last chapter). Recall that approximately 1 in 5 US adults has had a history of mental illness. Only a small proportion of these individuals suffer such dysfunction to the point they become homeless, and only a small proportion of those who become homeless decompensate psychiatrically to the point of being homeless, angry, and disheveled on the street. This person therefore represents a subset of a subset of a subset of people with mental illness.

But as a result, the highly visible person with mental illness in this scenario becomes closely associated with the public's mental picture of "mental illness" to a degree that is exaggerated because, in reality, these individuals are exceptional cases. At the same time, this means that mental illness experienced by the vast majority of people, whose mental illness remains hidden to most, factors less closely than it should into what society views as "mental illness."

Current stigma against people with mental illness can be traced throughout history. While mental illness for a long time was believed to originate in supernatural curses or possessions, the idea that mental illness was a medical disorder based in the body emerged in classical Greece and Rome, with, respectively, the work of the physicians Hippocrates and Galen.[41] However, the decline of the Greek and Roman medical model led to attributing mental illness to demonic possession, and, eventually, to sin during the Middle Ages. The humane and holistic practices of Hippocrates and Galen gave way to moral suasion, physical punishment, and incarceration, with some exceptions of more compassionate charitable care in Christian monasteries.[33] Meanwhile, the Arab world, along with preserving and enhancing Western knowledge generally during the medieval period, developed a rational, holistic, and comprehensive system of psychiatry, including asylums, parts of which Europe would adopt after the Enlightenment.[33,41]

Psychiatry in 1600s and 1700s Europe and America regarded some people with mental illness as irrational and therefore dangerous, tormenting them with treatments like spinning chairs, cold-water dunking, bleeding, and purging while confined in asylums. Fortunately, in the early 1800s, reformers such as Philippe Pinel in France and William Tuke in England, and later Dorothea Dix in America, began the movement away from punitive moral treatment and toward compassionate, respectful care.

The late 19th century saw improvements in treatment and diagnostic classifications, as well as Sigmund Freud's creation of psychoanalysis. Psychiatric medicines made slow progress until the 1950s, when their effectiveness helped many with mental illness live outside of asylums and in local communities, though too often without adequate support. Psychoanalysis, psychotherapy, and medication, increasingly offered in outpatient settings, gradually brought psychiatry out of remote asylums and into everyday life. Controversies persist, however, around involuntary treatment, diagnostic classification, pharmacological interventions, incarceration, and access to care.

This brief history shows that it has always been challenging to suffer mental illness, more so in some eras than in others. Indeed, to modern eyes, some approaches of the past appear ignorant, primitive, and teeming with stigma, though many citizens at the time probably thought them correct. No culture is without its blind spots and biases, and few within any culture have ever been eager to characterize their world negatively. Today we have unparalleled knowledge about science, medicine, psychology, neuroscience, social welfare, and health and wellness; nevertheless, social stigma of mental illness persists.

Social Stigma, Scapegoating, and Mental Illness

In a seminal article on stigma and mental illness, psychologist Patrick Corrigan and colleagues describe the factors that contribute to the public perceptions about people with mental illness, including that they are viewed as dangerous.[42] They describe the conceptual model of sociologists Bruce Link and Jo Phelan,[43] who "defined stigma with four components: (a) It is fundamentally a label of an out-group; (b) the labeled differences are negative; (c) the differences separate 'us' from 'them'; and (d) label and separation lead to status loss and discrimination."[42(p42)]

This framework posits that essential to understanding social stigma of people with mental illness is the implicit notion that "we" (those without mental illness) are not "them" (those with mental illness). Henri Tajfel, the mid-20th-century sociologist related this belief to an individual's social identity: "part of an individual's self-concept which derives from his knowledge of his membership of a social group (or groups) together with the emotional significance attached to that membership."[44(p69)] In addition, Tajfel noted that "the characteristics of one's group as a whole (such as its status, its richness or poverty, its skin color or its ability to reach its aims) achieve most of their significance in relation to perceived differences from other groups and the value connotation of these differences."[45(p71)]

But notice this process of stigmatizing "others" is not merely a separation of the groups. There is an additional part for "them" to be perceived negatively, as less worthy or less valuable as human beings. In *Upheavals of Thought*, philosopher Martha Nussbaum highlights the interplay between nature and nurture in her discussion of disgust, a feeling closely related to stigma, subordination, and exclusion:

> Disgust appears not to be present in infants during the first three years of life. It is taught by parents and society. This does not show that it does not have an evolutionary origin; many traits based on innate equipment take time to mature. But it does show that with disgust, as with language, social teaching plays a large role in shaping the form that the innate equipment takes. Usually this teaching begins during toilet training; ideas of indirect and psychological contamination are usually not firm until much later. Both parental and social teaching are involved in these developments.[46(p204)]

The roots of stigma can be shaped by significant social dynamics, family, and culture. If society feels disgust toward a group of individuals, then this implicitly separates and denigrates this group,[43,47] and these beliefs can be taught and passed down from generation to generation. So, to think and feel special about being a mentally healthy person, one must see themselves as separate from others with mental illness while also devaluing them—all the while having these attitudes reinforced by society to maintain such beliefs.

Another component of stigma is unpredictability,[43] suggested in the earlier example about encountering a psychotic person on the street. If it is difficult to predict the actions of another, one will not feel enough safety or confidence to enter into a cooperative relationship with that person, further exacerbating social exclusion. Building on understanding people stigmatized by mental illness, it is not merely that people with mental illness are separated from "us" and are perceived as less valuable than "us": because they are less predictable, they are also perceived as more dangerous than "us." According to psychologists Robert Kurzban and Mark Leary, over centuries, stigma and social exclusion may have provided adaptive advantages to social groups: "Everything else being equal, people with conditions that . . . connote greater danger are more stigmatized."[48(p190)]

Perceived connections between danger and mental illness are not new. This link is implicit in Ecclesiastes 9:3: "The hearts of men are full of evil, and madness is in their hearts while they live, and after that they go to the dead," and explicit in Herodotus's discussion of two accounts of violence by Persian King Cambyses II against his sister (kicking her during pregnancy and capricious execution): "These two crimes were committed against his own kin; both were the acts of a madman."[49]

This combination of factors contributing to the social stigmatizing of people with mental illness opens the door for the issues related to blame. As Corrigan and colleagues indicate, stereotyping and prejudice against people with mental illness can be seen in public beliefs that "people with mental illness are dangerous, incompetent, to *blame* for their disorder, unpredictable."[42(p42)]

But critically, the authors point out that stereotypes and prejudice also affect beliefs of people with mental illness themselves: "I am dangerous, incompetent, to *blame*."[42(p42)] Social stigma encompasses not only the ideas that people with mental illness are different from us, less than us, and more dangerous than us but also the idea that they are to blame for their condition. With respect to mental illness and violence, the message is this: "They" (people with mental illness) are to blame for "our" (people without mental illness) major social problem of violence.

For this reason, social stigma of mental illness relates to the concept of scapegoating—singling out a person or group of people for undeserved blame. The Old Testament Book of Leviticus spells out several different forms of purification and atonement involving the ritual sacrifice of bulls, goats, and rams:

And when he has made an end of atoning for the holy place and the tent of meeting and the altar, he shall present the live goat; and Aaron shall lay both his hands upon the head of the live goat, and confess over him all the iniquities of the people of Israel, and all their transgressions, all their sins; and he shall put them upon the head of the goat, and send him away into the wilderness by the hand of a man who is in readiness. The goat shall bear all their iniquities upon him to a solitary land; and he shall let the goat go in the wilderness.[50(p102)]

In classical Greece, the scapegoat was not an animal but an undesirable person:

A man, generally a criminal, was led around through the streets, fed, flogged with green branches, and finally expelled or killed. He was called pharmakos, which is the masculine form of pharmakon (medicine). Some scholars regard the pharmakos as a scapegoat on whom the sins and the impurity of the people were loaded and who was then expelled or destroyed.[51(p23)]

The ancient Greek use of the same word for "scapegoat" and "medicine" mixed beliefs and rituals about purification with those of medicine with lasting mythopoetic force and helps show how the scapegoating of people with mental illness and confusion about their conditions and treatment persist even in modern societies that ought to know better. As commentators have noted with respect to social stigma of mental illness, "Not only have we inherited a tendency to respond to crises by scapegoating, but we have also evolved a cognitive bias towards selectively scapegoating people who are mentally ill. In other words, our evolutionary origins make us prone to the fallacious conclusion that 'if something is wrong, the madman must be responsible.'"[52(p505)]

Ultimately, this social stigma and scapegoating have fueled exaggeration of the link between violence and mental illness. Prejudices and biases that people with mental illness are a separate group of people to be blamed for violence is seen today in news reports and popular media, as well as in use of a language of dehumanization. The general public remain vulnerable to adopting misinformation, uncertainty, fear, and stigma regarding people who suffer from mental illness because this belief is frequently reinforced in society and popular culture.

Exaggeration about Violence and Mental Illness in News Media

After mass shootings or notable acts of violence in America, the news media highlights speculation about the mental health status of the perpetrator. For those with the interest and patience to follow and think about the stories of mass shooters or violent perpetrators over periods of time, the initial media overreaction and its scapegoating of mental illness is sometimes corrected but only gradually. For those who are drawn to the horror of immediate news but who lose interest as the story slows, that scapegoating can more easily be perceived as fact.

Mass shootings are terrifying, anomalous events demanding a quick scapegoat, and the news media frequently offers up mental illness as the cause, as if it were a knee-jerk reaction. The impact of the overreaction on public opinion is clear. In the aftermath of a mass shooting at the Washington Navy Yard in which a lone gunman killed 12 people, a Gallup poll conducted in September 2013 showed that "forty-eight percent of Americans blame the mental health system 'a great deal' for mass shootings in the United States, unchanged from January 2011. At the same time, fewer blame easy access to guns now (40%) than two years ago (46%), *making the mental health system the perceived top cause of mass shootings.*"[53]

The trend of mental illness being blamed more often than gun access has continued in public perception in the United States. A 2022 Monmouth University poll found: "When asked which factor is more responsible for the number of recent mass shootings in the US, 55% say it is a mental health crisis in the country while 33% say the ease of getting guns is more to blame."[54] Mental health, and by proxy mental illness, continues to be perceived as the top cause of violence.

When news media bestow upon mass killers like Adam Lanza, perpetrator of the 2012 Sandy Hook Elementary School massacre in Newtown, Connecticut, hypothetical diagnoses like schizophrenia, they are trying to explain and expel the incomprehensible for a startled and anxious populace but in the context of having limited evidence. As scholars have pointed out,[12] in the aftermath of this horrific school shooting, voices as varied as New York Governor Andrew Cuomo ("People who have mental health issues should not have guns."), National Rifle Association

President Wayne LaPierre ("delusional killers"), and conservative commentator Ann Coulter ("Guns don't kill people—the mentally ill do.") joined *Psychology Today* ("Was Adam Lanza an undiagnosed schizophrenic?") and the *New York Times* ("Lanza's acts of slaughter . . . strongly suggest undiagnosed schizophrenia.") in suggesting that shooter Adam Lanza's history of psychosis—featuring a speculative, posthumous diagnosis of schizophrenia offered by those who had never assessed him—caused the murder of 20 children and six adults.

But after one of the most extensive investigations of a mass murderer ever conducted in history, Adam Lanza was *never* found to have schizophrenia. The final report of the Sandy Hook Advisory Commission in 2015 concluded: "Experts who contributed to that report found insufficient evidence to suggest that he would have qualified for a psychotic illness."[55(p70)]

News media do present crimes and murders with more consideration of multiple causes of violence in the context of less sensational violent crimes. To illustrate, according to the local news station in the Piedmont region of North Carolina,[56] Jonathan Sander of Wake Forest, North Carolina, was convicted in the 2019 murder of his business partner with a shotgun after a dispute over the dissolution of their lawn care business. He also was alleged to have shot and killed his business partner's wife and his mother.

The news report indicated that Mr. Sander had a long history of heavy alcohol and marijuana use, bipolar disorder, and interpersonal hostility and conflicts. Adding to the tragedy, Mr. Sander was reported to be under financial strain and had actually sought psychiatric help prior to the murders but received none because he could not afford it.

WRAL.com followed the case closely, with reporter Matthew Burns providing sober, measured reporting on Mr. Sander's drug abuse, psychiatric history, conflicts with his business partner, and his legal and financial problems, including video clips of a forensic psychiatrist and a forensic psychologist offering testimony regarding Mr. Sander's mental status and pertinent stressors around the time of the shootings.

Though the reports could have delved more into Mr. Sander's access to a loaded gun and lack of access to psychiatric treatment during a critical and dangerous point in his life, overall, the coverage dispassionately presented the information a reader would need to develop a rational view of the combination of factors that led Mr. Sander to murder three people. Multiple violence risk factors were offered as contributing to the violent acts.

Although it is true that Mr. Sander had a history of mental illness, he also had multiple other even more significant risk factors for violence, including abusing drugs and alcohol, being male, having access to a gun, and facing serious legal and financial challenges. Why was the news media better able to sidestep scapegoating mental illness with Jonathan Sander? One could speculate that because Jonathan Sander, unlike Adam Lanza, killed three people in a manner that people understood was not a threat to them because the victims were known to the perpetrator. Conversely, Adam Lanza killed multiple strangers, most of them children, in a relatively rare, incomprehensible slaughter, reminding nearly everyone that such a thing could happen to them, or, even worse, to their children.

Such horrific events trigger a need for explanation: given the components of social stigma of mental illness highlighted above, these events become a go-to cause for incomprehensible and terror-based violence. And yet crimes such as domestic violence and child abuse, more prevalent than mass murder, receive far less attention in the news media and therefore remain relatively invisible. Instead, mental illness has been portrayed negatively and disproportionately mentioned in conjunction with violence in the news for decades.[57-59]

Exaggeration about Violence and Mental Illness in Popular Media

News media patterns of pointing to mental illness in its reports of mass shootings are not the products of journalism alone. They also receive ongoing reinforcement from popular media. Horror films, for example, exploit primitive fears of lurking irrational violence. Anthropologist Shawn M. Phillips has noted that horror films featuring slashers or serial killers depict those characters as having congenital physical or mental disorders as marks of deviancy which define the characters and their motives while also comforting the audience:

Thus atrocities can be observed and enjoyed from the comfortable distance of mass entertainment while boundaries are maintained between the audience, the deviant acts, and the perpetrators. Most importantly, the uniform reaction of disgust and horror confirms the normalcy of the audience against the disabled portrayed as deviants in this genre.[60(p65)]

This connects to Nussbaum's concept of disgust and how it contributes to separating "us" without mental illness from "them" with mental illness by devaluing the latter to further social stigma. In horror films, as in the mass news media's biased reports of mass shooters with mental illness, "Notions of horror and deviance replace the need for substantial issues such as motive. If the disabled can be classed as deviants, then we need know nothing more about them because their boundary violation is sufficient."[60]

Nonetheless, films are just one medium in which social stigma of people with mental illness is perpetuated, along with books, newspapers, television, magazines, radio, advertising, internet, and social media. Mental illness in the popular media, for many people, brings to mind compulsively homicidal characters like Hannibal Lecter in Thomas Harris's *Silence of the Lambs*. In the TV series *Game of Thrones*, Daenerys Targaryen transforms into the "Mad Queen" only after she commits a horrific and prolonged act of mass murder. In the preface of the 2003 printing of his 1995 book, *Media Madness*,[61] psychologist Otto Wahl describes how popular media continues to distort mental illness:

Despite some notable exceptions (e.g. Oscar winner *A Beautiful Mind*), little has changed in the way of media depiction of mental illnesses since *Media Madness* was published. Examples could be updated, but basic themes remain the same. *Hunter* and *Kojak* and *Police Story* may have left the air, but other detective dramas have followed, with their own connections of mental illness and violence. *Law and Order* has remained— and expanded into additional spin-offs—continuing the representation of people with mental illnesses as criminals and villains. Norman Bates may no longer be the prototypical Hollywood *Psycho*, but Hannibal (The Cannibal) Lecter has captured the movie going public's imagination with his disturbed and disturbing villainy. *Halloween*'s escaped mental patient Michael Myers has continued to slice and dice his way through sequels to his twentieth anniversary in *H2O* and his *Resurrection* in 2002. Sitcoms have come and gone, but whatever their titles, they find ways to present mental illnesses as ridiculous and laughable. *Seinfeld's* crazy Joe Davoli and *The Simpsons'* Sideshow Bob live on in syndication, while *Frasier* continues to make disparaging remarks about the troubled listeners who call his radio show.[61(pXI)]

The stories of relentless, remorseless murderers, despite their lurid appeal, tell us very little about violence, mental illness, or the connection between the two. Yet they do reveal how stigma and bias about mental illness can be used to horrify the general public.

While there is a long history of mental illness being portrayed negatively and misrepresented in all those media, the media can feature sympathetic depictions in which the protagonists' mental disorders become akin to "superpowers" that account for their professional success. Detective Adrian Monk (actor Tony Shalhoub) in *Monk* (obsessive-compulsive disorder, multiple phobias), Dr. Gregory House (Hugh Laurie) in *House, M.D.* (depression, opiate abuse), and FBI special agent Will Graham (Hugh Dancy) in *Hannibal* (superhuman ability to empathize with anyone) outperform and amaze their crime-fighting peers and contemporaries in medical practice because their symptoms are their superpowers.

Because these latter depictions do not blame mental illness for violence and do not portray mental illness in a negative light, they do not necessarily contribute to social stigma of mental illness as described above. Nevertheless, these depictions also do not provide an accurate portrayal of mental illness either. Mental illnesses do not confer such superpowers, but instead are associated with loss of concentration and reduced cognitive function. Further, in some of these shows, a hidden message is that mental health treatment is not beneficial; namely, when these characters' symptoms are diminished with medications or therapy, the characters become less effective (i.e., their superpowers diminish along with the symptoms). But this misses the opportunity to communicate that people with mental illness suffer when they experience symptoms and feel dramatic relief from stress, pain, and suffering when properly treated.

Exaggeration about Violence and Mental Illness and Language of Dehumanization

In his book *Less than Human*, David Livingstone Smith describes how language and labeling can be used to separate groups such as people with mental illness into "us" versus "them."[62] He writes that a "tactic is to call these people 'sick'—that is, those with mental illness. Surely, one might think, anyone who performs such terrible, brutal acts, or orders them to be done, has got to be severely psychologically disturbed." [62(p136)]

Such language and labels do not comport with the evidence, as Smith recounts how Nazi war criminals "were often touted as paradigmatic examples of genocidal *madmen*."[62(p136)] But evidence disputes that mental illness is to blame. Smith relates the findings of psychiatrist Leon Goldensohn, who provided psychiatric care to Nazi war criminals and concluded "the defendants at Nuremberg were anything but mentally ill."[62(p136)]

Similarly, Smith states that Islamist extremist militants have been equated with "moral *insanity*."[62(p136)] But again, evidence disputes that mental illness is to blame. Smith relates findings of the researcher Marc Sageman, who interviewed hundreds of Islamist extremist militants and found "no obvious mental health problems."[62(p136)] Smith concludes that even though language can be used to exaggerate a link to violence and mental illness, this language is not grounded in science.[62]

Such language of dehumanization can be used to further stigmatize people with mental illness. For example, in August 2019, there were multiple mass shootings in El Paso, Texas, and Dayton, Ohio. After the El Paso and Dayton shootings, politicians' reactions included labeling those who commit mass shootings "mentally ill monsters."[63] Considering there is no evidence proving that murderous hatred is a symptom of mental illness, this reaction to mass violence mirrored and reinforced its deep intransigence in the public mind. Linking mental illness to monsters separates "us" from "them" by devaluing "them." But it goes one step further: devaluing people with mental illness to the extent that they do not count as people and are not even classified as human beings.

Importantly, the Dayton shooter was killed by police at the scene of the crime, and the detained El Paso shooter had not been formally evaluated by a psychologist or a psychiatrist, rendering the mental status of either during their crimes mere speculation. Additionally, terrorist behavior, unlike the behavior of people with acute psychiatric symptoms, is in most cases organized, coherent, and planned, no matter what one may think of its purpose, morality, or underlying ideology. "Mentally ill monsters" and use of other labels—vermin, excrement, disease, contagion, and predation—transforms humans into subhumans. Dehumanizing language facilitates what David Livingstone Smith calls "moral disengagement," after which even otherwise sensible and loving people can rationalize designating others as nonhumans.[62]

The expression "mentally ill monsters" goes beyond "them" versus "us" because it makes "them" nonhuman. "Monsters," even further, have embodied everything humans find dangerous and terrifying, including creatures from mythology and religion throughout history. Of course, most contemporary people know better. Monsters are not real. But use of dehumanizing metaphors can be used to falsely convince many that people with mental illness are predators who pose a specific, potent, nonhuman threat to the public, thereby adding another layer of prejudice and risk of harm to an already disadvantaged and often mistreated group of people.

What are the unintended consequences of stigma, scapegoating, and the language of dehumanization? Consider a person experiencing mental health symptoms but who does not want to be seen as "mentally ill" because of the stigma attached to this label we have just described. Is this person more or less likely to seek out treatment for those mental health symptoms before the symptoms increase? This person may be less likely to seek out treatment due to stigma, a finding confirmed by empirical research.[64,65] But what is the effect? This could foreseeably adversely impact their social functioning, their ability to keep a job, to keep financial security. And it could elevate the chances a person self-medicates with alcohol or another substance. Ironically, the social stigma associated with mental illness can be traced in this case to increasing risk factors for violent behavior. But note that the increased risk is not due to the mental illness itself but from widespread social stigma and bias against people with mental illness.

Placing blame for violence on "them" involves shifting attention away from the risk of violence that exists among everyone in the general public who has other risk factors. In August 2019, the National Council for Behavioral Health issued the report "Mass Violence in America: Causes, Impacts, and Solutions"[66] and was clear about the dangers of singling out people with mental illness:

> Profiling is especially problematic when the suggestion is made to screen all people with mental health problems to prevent rare acts of serious violence. The danger is that those who are identified as being at risk of violence, rather than being given priority access to treatment and becoming eligible for intensive services, will instead be discriminated against, deprived of their liberty and subject to social control, whether through arrest and incarceration or involuntary inpatient or outpatient commitment. *In addition, when only people with mental illnesses are profiled, many others who might commit violence are missed.*[66(p17)]

When dehumanizing language like "mentally ill monsters" is used and amplified throughout the media, stigma expands. If people with mental illness are blamed for violence, and the link to violence is exaggerated to be stronger than it is, then society will inaccurately discount other factors as less strong and fail to identify people who do not have mental illness and pose a much greater threat.

In sum, socially stigmatizing mental illness necessitates separating people into groups of "them" versus "us." We see this stigmatization is not only about how people with mental illness are seen as different and devalued but also about how mental illness is blamed for violence, enabling scapegoating about the role of mental illness in causing society's troubles—recall the Gallup and Monmouth polls showing mental illness as the top perceived cause of violence.

Outsize acts of violence like mass shootings will always be shocking and upsetting, especially to those who experience them firsthand and their families. Even in contemporary America, where mass shootings are tragically occurring now with greater regularity, the public has not yet fully accepted them, thankfully, as a normal part of life. And though such acts are initially unfathomable, they do not have to remain that way if people strive to understand these acts beyond automatic and immediate, yet scientifically unfounded, blaming of mental illness. Social stigma has reinforced links between violence and mental illness, and as we will see in the next chapter, cognitive biases also play a key role.

3

Cognitive Biases and Exaggerations about
Mental Illness and Violence

In the past few decades, social psychologists and behavioral economists have studied how human beings make judgments, predictions, and decisions in the face of uncertain information or incomplete information, such as when we try to figure out whether a person will become violent. In social psychological research, experiments may involve presenting study participants with a scenario and questions. Derived from a study published in the field of law and psychology,[67] consider the following data and questions:

> Between 1970 and 1972 in the state of Wyoming, there were 26,567 persons arrested and 22,102 indicted for felonies. During this period, how many defendants raised the insanity defense? And when the insanity defense was raised, in how many cases was it successful?

For facts like this that are not well known, social psychologists hypothesize that people rely on mental shortcuts called "heuristics" to help them arrive at an estimate. Heuristics draw on a person's past experiences and knowledge in specific ways. These are the cognitive lenses through which we perceive the world.

Write down your answers before reading ahead. This scenario was used in a psychology experiment[67] investigating how the public viewed the insanity defense and the perceived links between violence and mental illness. On average, the participants in the study estimated that the insanity defense was raised 8,151 times. This means of the 22,102 felony indictments, the participants guessed the insanity defense was raised more than once for every three defendants, 37% of the time. The median was 8,840.75, meaning about half the sample postulated more than this number, and half believed it was less. There was a wide range of estimates, too, with participants responding that the insanity defense was raised between 30 to 25,000 times. When asked about how successful the insanity defense was, the participants guessed that during the period studied it was successful a little less than half the time. This result translated to 44% of these defendants being acquitted, the mean estimate being 3,599 successful insanity defenses.

Compare your answers with those numbers. The actual numbers? Between 1970 and 1972, of 26,567 persons arrested and 22,102 indicted for felonies in the state of Wyoming, *the insanity defense was raised 108 times and was successful once.*[67] This figure is, of course, much lower than the study participants' estimates.

Admittedly, this is one state during one period of time. Insanity defense rates do fluctuate in different US states. A review across many states in 1994 showed that the insanity defense is raised approximately 0.9% of the time and successful about one-quarter of the time.[68] To our knowledge, there have been no new studies with updated figures. Nevertheless, as of 2022, in the state of North Carolina, there were about 30,000 inmates housed in 57 prisons whereas there were 76 forensic beds in 1 mental health facility to house individuals found not guilty by reason of insanity (though not all these beds are for this purpose but also for individuals found incapable to proceed to trial). The ratio is approximately 2.4 forensic patients per 1,000 offenders criminally convicted, showing again that the former group constitutes a minuscule amount compared to the latter group. Overall, these numbers reveal a substantial gap between the perception of the insanity defense and its reality. What should we take from these studies and statistics? Mental illness is far less often the primary cause of violence and crime than people think.

But what about when people are asked whether someone with mental illness is dangerous? In 2019, sociologists Bernice Pescosolido and Bianca Manago and law professor John Monahan analyzed the National Stigma Studies (part of the National Opinion Research Center's General Social Survey), tracking levels of public stigma regarding people with mental illness over three points in time, 1996, 2006, and 2018.[69] As background, the authors discussed research data from the 1950s. They found that the public had become more knowledgeable about the causes and varieties of mental illness over time. Yet the evidence also revealed that by 1996, people were significantly more likely to mention violence when asked to define mental illness spontaneously.

When the authors examined data from 1996 to 2018, *the studies showed increases in public perception that people with mental illness were likely to be dangerous* and in public support for involuntary treatment.[69] For example, in 1996, about 57% rated that it was "likely" that a person with schizophrenia would "do something violent toward other people." By contrast, in 2018, about 67% had the same response. This finding is at odds with research showing the exact opposite: most people with schizophrenia and other mental illnesses are not violent.[23] Moreover, the finding implies increases in public fear of people with mental illness and a concurrent greater tolerance for involuntary hospitalization. As Pescosolido, Manago, and Monahan conclude in their analysis of the Stigma Studies:

> Emboldened by political arguments, daily reports of impersonal violence, and media mentions linking mental illness and crime, members of the public may be expected to continue to support the stigma of dangerousness and call for the return of mental asylums as suggested recently by politicians. Undertaking efforts to counteract these sources of stigma is daunting but indispensable to public health. We caution against policies based on erroneously linking mental illness and violence. Public policies stoked by political rhetoric will not improve the lives of any Americans.[69(p1742)]

Research on Cognitive Biases Applied to Perceptions of Mental Illness and Violence

As described in the previous chapter, long-standing social stigma and bias against people with mental illness fueling perceptions that they are dangerous, in addition to skewed portrayals of mental illness by news and mass media,[70] all work together to perpetuate the belief that many violent acts are caused by mental illness. The above finding from the National Stigma Study confirms that this belief is, in fact, widespread, with two-thirds of the public surveyed rating a hypothetical person diagnosed with schizophrenia as dangerous. Even more troubling, these views appear to have become more entrenched in the United States over the past few decades. The advent and expansion of the DSM over the same period do not appear to have mitigated stigma against people with mental illness.

Public misperceptions about mental illness and violence are harmful because they feed prejudice against a vulnerable group of individuals who are much more likely to hurt themselves than others and more likely to be victims of violence than people without mental illness. At a minimum, participants' responses regarding the frequency of the insanity defense reveal an exaggeration of the proportion of criminal behavior that the public perceives involves mental illness. It also shows the magnitude by which the public believes mental illness is responsible for criminal behavior. At its core, the message is clear: the public believes mental illness is to blame for a lot more crime than is actually the case.

This misperception arguably stems from cognitive biases that reinforce one another. Examining conceptions of stigma provides a context for how the misperception that people with mental illness are violent has been perpetuated throughout history and by the media. Yet why do these misperceptions remain so resistant to change, especially in an increasingly psychologically minded culture? Social psychological research has identified many cognitive biases that underlie much of our thinking. We contend that people are vulnerable to several biases and distortions when violence occurs. Below we examine how a combination of cognitive biases can perpetuate stigma and the belief that people with mental illness are violent.

At least three reactions occur when people are confronted with news about violence: (1) they want to understand and explain what caused the heinous act, (2) people focus on the perpetrator and their individual reasons for the violence, and (3) people want to do something about it and produce a solution to prevent violence from occurring again. The problem is that amid intense emotional reactions to violence, people are vulnerable to what Nobel Prize–winning psychologist Daniel Kahneman refers to as "thinking fast" in an emotional and non-reflective way, which leads to cognitive biases.[71] Instead, a person can engage in what Kahneman refers to as "thinking slow" in a logical and deliberative way to evaluate the violence accurately and to counterbalance cognitive biases.

For the first reaction, in which people want to understand and explain what caused the heinous act, people consider and recall causes of violence. Research shows that in this situation, people "think fast" and often rely on what is called the "availability heuristic" in which people think something is important because it is readily accessible to memory. Given that the media regularly offers mental illness as the explanation for a violent act, this risk factor is recalled quickly. As a result, the link between violence and mental illness is inaccurately perceived as more prominent than it is. To counterbalance this and "think slow," a person would gather more information on the multiple factors precipitating a perpetrator's violent act, not just the information available immediately after it.

For the second reaction, in which people focus on the perpetrator and their reasons for the violence, people "thinking fast" tend to overweigh individual-level variables and to discount environment-level variables when evaluating other people's behavior, which is a cognitive bias called the "fundamental attribution error." This suggests that individual-level variables like a person's mental illness are more likely to be blamed for violence than such environmental-level risk factors as the perpetrator being a member of an online hate group, inadequate family and social support, childhood physical abuse, financial strain, or having access to guns and semiautomatic assault rifles. To "think slow," a person would recognize the role of the environment in shaping human behavior along with individual-level factors like mental illness and then consider environment-level elements like social networks, financial strain, and gun access.

For the third reaction, in which people want to do something about it and produce a solution to prevent violence from occurring again, people prefer explanations that confer an ability to control a solution called the "theater of control." Many in the public "think fast" and without much reflection, jump to the conclusion that mental health professionals could have prevented the violence. But when one "thinks slow" about this solution, they would recognize that there are no methods to read the minds of patients who may have violent thoughts, no perfect assessments to predict violence, and no proven drugs to prevent violence. Below, we discuss each of these three reactions in more detail, along with their related cognitive biases and how to correct them.

The Impetus to Explain Violent Acts and the Availability Heuristic

Extreme acts of violence, graphically reported across a 24-hour news media cycle, are traumatic reminders of the fragility of life. Humans are naturally very keen to manage threats to that fragility. After hearing about the horror of such events, many will respond with a strong urge to grasp what caused the violence, to automatically calculate any risk of such a thing happening to them, and how to prevent it. The reaction to try to understand what motivated the violence is reasonable. Violence shatters the sense of safety and security people rely upon to live their lives.

For most people, the information available to understand violence is transmitted by the news media and popular culture. Mental illness is mentioned quickly and a disproportionate number of times in the vast majority of media reports about violence, even when the perpetrator may not have a mental illness.[72] This nearly universal media reaction to violence affects the public's focus on mental illness when violence occurs. As described above, mental illness is frequently the first piece of information, whether inaccurate or problematic, made available to the public. And because that information is so readily accessible, it promotes mental illness as a "usual suspect" in identifying an immediate, primary, or even singular cause for the violence.

What is the impact of frequently blaming mental illness as the primary cause of well-publicized violence? This repeated cycle of violence and repeated initial consideration of mental illness can lead to the availability heuristic.[71] The availability heuristic describes situations in "which people assess the frequency of a class or probability of an event by the ease with which instances or occurrences can be brought to mind."[71(p425)] In other words, a piece of information is weighed more if it is easier to bring to mind. Kahneman explains that availability leads to predictable biases because it is influenced by factors other than probability:

> The risk involved in an adventurous expedition, for example, is evaluated by imagining contingencies in which the expedition is not equipped to cope. If many such difficulties are vividly portrayed, the expedition can

appear exceedingly dangerous, although the ease with which disasters are imagined need not reflect their actual likelihood. Conversely, the risk involved in an undertaking may be grossly underestimated if some possible dangers are either difficult to conceive of, or simply do not come to mind.[71(p426)]

Substitute the many vivid portrayals in the media of people with mental illness as violent and the frequent blaming of mental illness for violence in the news. The availability heuristic would therefore predict bias toward overestimating individuals with mental illness as dangerous. Conversely, consider violence risk factors less frequently portrayed in the news and media, such as younger age, being male, alcohol abuse, lacking empathy, and antisocial personality disorder. The availability heuristic would therefore predict bias toward underestimating the strength of these risk factors.

Kahneman describes another form of the availability heuristic relevant to blaming violence on mental illness: "illusory correlation."[71] This bias occurs when two pieces of information are frequently mentioned together. This phenomenon leads to a bias that they are correlated. In a famous experiment by psychologists Loren and Jean Chapman, study participants were asked about hypothetical patients with psychiatric disorders.[73] They read information about a mental health diagnosis and a drawing of a person by that patient. Later in the experiment, participants were asked to rate how frequently they thought a mental health diagnosis (e.g., paranoid ideation) was accompanied by atypical aspects of a drawing (e.g., peculiar depiction of eyes). The result? Participants overestimated the co-occurrence of a mental health diagnosis and unusual parts of the picture even though this correlation was completely fictitious.

Applied to the exaggeration of mental illness and violence, the media's frequent *concurrent* mention of violence and mental illness means this information is readily available to the public, even if incorrect. It reinforces the illusory correlation between the two, fueling an exaggerated close association between violence and mental illness. Often, politicians or family members of the perpetrators parrot media assertions about mental illness as the cause, adding to the availability heuristic. Thus, a foundation is set up regarding how the public reacts to acts of violence and relies on the availability heuristic to be more likely to perceive violence as the act of a person with mental illness.

Since relatively few people commit excessive violence, most people cannot comprehend what could motivate another person to commit such acts. As described in the previous chapter, the public may attribute such alien actions to individuals who must be starkly different—people with mental illness, thereby separating the "sane us" from the "insane them." This process further feeds the belief that it must have been a mental illness that caused the violence. The availability heuristic concludes that if the perpetrator has mental health problems, then that must be why they would commit something like a mass shooting. Case closed.

However, it is virtually always unknown, especially early on, whether mental illness is ever diagnosed in the perpetrator. Instead, there is speculation in the initial days following a violent incident. Nevertheless, this lack of actual data is largely ignored. At the same time, the public and policymakers extend the availability heuristic to rapid consideration of other related pieces of evidence, however small, that showed the perpetrator may have "mental health issues." A friend or family member says the perpetrator had been anxious, depressed, or angry. But ignored is the fact the vast majority of people have felt these emotions at some point in their lives.

Another way mental illness can be blamed for violence is if it is learned that the perpetrator may have been prescribed psychotropic medications. But ignored is the fact that psychotropic medications are widely prescribed for common problems, such as Valium for people afraid of flying in an airplane. As a result, the ubiquity of mental health symptoms makes retrofitting these as the cause of violence easy, even if there is no evidence to make such a strong and instant connection. It also contributes to mental illness being quickly raised as an initial cause of violence and therefore increasing the likelihood that the next time violence occurs, mental illness will quickly be brought to mind as the cause.

When it comes to violence reported in the news, the illusory correlation is at play. While violence and mental illness are discussed together, the many more potent risk factors unreported and unavailable to the public go unidentified as causes of violence. Studies show that there is a disproportionate amount of news media devoted to violence and mental illness.[57] When violence happens, it is rarer for the news to report about the person abusing substances, being unemployed, or angry about a turn in their life they could not control, even though these are likely contributors to violence. Rarely will the news point out that the perpetrator is young and male, even though these are among the strongest predictors of violence. As a result, in its efforts to understand violence, the public is limited to picking a few of the usual suspects, too often mental illness, and therefore vulnerable to exaggeration consistent with the illusory correlation. Also missing from much of the news are the millions more violent acts that are rarely publicized because they are not unusual, such as domestic violence, sexual assault, armed robbery, and aggravated assault.

Mental health experts who routinely assess violence risk are not immune to the availability heuristic. Research shows that mental health clinicians consider firmly established risk factors (e.g., details about violence history) less frequently when these variables are less accessible.[74] Conversely, researchers found that clinicians working in an inpatient psychiatric facility prioritized recent violent behaviors (in the hospital) over past violence (before hospital admission) in their judgments of patients' violence risk, reflecting this bias in human information processing to favor recent, more easily accessed data.[75] Similarly, studies have found that the broad domain of risk factors that were most readily available to clinicians in practice (e.g., psychiatric diagnosis) are rated as the most relevant whereas the risk factors that were less available (e.g., childhood history) are seen as less relevant by clinicians.[74,76] Finally, researchers have noted that clinicians, like the study participants in the Chapman and Chapman study, often focus on salient cues (e.g., bizarre paranoid delusional beliefs) that may not actually be related to a person's violent behavior at all.[77] Keep in mind that mental health professionals do not have the ability to predict violence perfectly. We will return to this at the end of the chapter.

For now, to avoid the availability heuristic with respect to violence and mental illness, we suggest that there needs to be a shift in how the public thinks about violence when it happens. Instead of immediately assuming mental illness as the cause, we need to recognize that there is much critical information lacking in the first 24–48 hours after an incident of violence and that any quick conclusion is likely flawed. Reflect on the fact that the insanity defense—which is predicated on a criminal trial in which the multiple causes of the violent act have had time to be gathered and reviewed in evidence—is rarely successful, attesting to the fact that rarely is mental illness found to be the primary or sole cause of violence. Thus, to avoid the trap of the availability heuristic when violence occurs, we must recall that there are definitely aspects of the perpetrator that will *not* be known immediately and may only become known if there is a criminal trial after the perpetrator is arrested, even when the defendant has mental illness. Rather than automatically asking "Did they have mental illness?" one could ask "What else was going on?" Then there needs to be further investigation about the perpetrator that goes beyond the first paragraph of a news article or a report released the day after the violent act.

The Impetus to Blame the Person for Violence and the Fundamental Attribution Error

Another important cognitive bias linked to violence and mental illness is called the "fundamental attribution error." To understand this, let us first discuss what "attribution" means in the context of identifying factors that cause human behavior. In 1936, psychologist Kurt Lewin proposed a relatively straightforward formula to describe the factors underlying human behavior, $B = f(P, E)$, which means that behavior is a function of the person and the person's environment.[78,79] The person includes what can be considered all aspects of an individual, including their past, present, expectations of the future, mental capacities, motivations, and desires. One's environment can include social, work, living, financial, and family domains. Applied to violence, Lewin's formula would postulate that violence results from an interaction of a person with their environment.

Yet the news rarely provides detailed information about a person's environment and instead provides more information about the individual because of easier accessibility. But the disproportionate mention of details about a person's suspected or alleged mental illness encourages this fundamental attribution error. This leads to overvaluing an individual's personal characteristics and undervaluing aspects of an individual's overall environment or social situation. A false dichotomy that ignores Lewin's formula is often promulgated by the media or politicians: it's the person that pulls the trigger, not the gun. But the existence of individual-level risk factors does not magically erase the existence of environmental-level risk factors. When it comes to explaining violence, the fundamental attribution error leads people to emphasize individual characteristics (e.g., mental illness) and to discount environmental variables (e.g., unemployment, poor social support, financial strain, marital strife, gun access) as contributing to a behavior.

This tendency is encouraged by news media's use of blunt, sensational headlines to attract clicks and views. Yet, that a person's environment has a significant impact on aggression and violence is well established. In the MacArthur Violence Risk Assessment Study, considered one of the gold standard investigations of violence to date, researchers found that living in disadvantaged or unsafe neighborhoods was associated with higher risk of violence, even when controlling for individual-level variables.[80] Another study similarly found that living in an environment in which an individual was exposed to violence itself increased risk that the person would act violently.[81] Research has confirmed that financial debt, unemployment, and lower income were all strong predictors of violence.[23] Ready access to weapons has also been shown to increase risk of violence, in particular domestic violence.[82] As commentators note with respect to violence and symptoms of mental illness, "The association between a particular set of clinical symptoms and violence does not preclude the possibility that both may be rooted in social factors originating external to the individual's mental state."[83(p63)]

Correspondingly, Eric Kandel writes about the role of one's environment in understanding violence and reviews animal research on the topic,[40] providing an example of fruit flies who fight with one another to obtain food and push against each other to achieve dominance. Kandel notes that both environment-level and individual-level factors influence aggression: "A fly that is isolated at the pupa stage and raised to adulthood in a vial is much more aggressive than flies that have been housed in groups."[40(p550)] He then expands on this observation, stating, "This is true throughout the animal kingdom—isolation breeds aggressiveness. The environment can also act by influencing the expression of genes . . . studies of hyperaggressive flies may one day yield insights into how genes control aggression and into the interaction between heredity and environment in producing aggression."[40(p550)]

Thus, scientific research shows that when "thinking slow" about violence it is important to keep Lewin's formula in mind and to seek information about a perpetrator's environment. Otherwise, our reasoning about what caused the violence will be skewed and erroneous, neglecting important contributing factors while wrongly over-ascribing causal attribution to less influential or extraneous factors. Given that people are prone to blaming behavior on the person and not their environment, and that media portrayals of violence and the DSM emphasize individual symptoms rather than social context, it is not surprising that the fundamental attribution error has been found even among skilled clinicians. In one study,[84] researchers examined clinicians' perceptions of violence risk and found that they overemphasized individual-level factors and gave the least weight to environmental-level variables (e.g., employment, social network, and financial situation).[84]

In another study,[76] mental health clinicians were asked to think about their patients and list the risk factors they thought were most important for assessing a patient's risk of violence. Of the over 1,080 risk factors listed by clinicians, 975 were categorized as focusing on individual-level variables; less than 10% concerned environment-level variables. When asked to rate the importance of risk factors listed in a survey, the top-five risk factors considered most relevant by clinicians were focused on individual-level characteristics—none were environmental level. Similarly, psychologists Michael Odeh, Robert Zeiss, and Matthew Huss[85] had clinicians rate risk factors for violence in more than 300 patient protocols and discovered that of the risk cues used, the vast majority were individual level with few related to contextual or situational factors.[85] As with the availability heuristic, mental health clinicians are not immune to the fundamental attribution error.

To avoid the trap of the fundamental attribution error regarding violence, it is essential not only to analyze the characteristics of the perpetrator but also the environment in which they lived. Were they unemployed or did they recently lose a job? Did they have substantial financial debt? Were they members of hate groups or a gang? How supportive were their family and friends? Did they have ready access to deadly weapons? Was the perpetrator recently a victim of violence? Did the perpetrator recently have a significant relationship end in separation or divorce? Where and how did they live? In an unsafe neighborhood with regular exposure to violence? These are additional questions to ask in order to rebalance Lewin's formula and remove the fundamental attribution error from the identification of risk factors for violence.

The Impetus to Prevent Future Violent Acts and Crime Control Theater

There is a third cognitive bias to address when violence occurs, and this originates from the impetus to arrive at a solution to prevent violence from repeating. Mental illness, unlike being young or male (two of the strongest predictors of violence), can be treated and, therefore, the public may be under the impression that this "cause" of violence is also something society can prevent. The idea persists that if the perpetrator had been in treatment, the event would not have occurred. The general public falls victim to biased or distorted thinking in the midst of intense emotional reactions, such as, "If only treatment would have happened, then violence could've been prevented." People then look for a quick policy fix to beef up violence prevention. This approach is consistent with the theory of Crime Control Theater,[86] which posits that some laws and policies are created to make people feel like someone is doing something, even though the action is ineffective and sometimes detrimental—mere theater or worse.

Lack of understanding that mental health professionals have limitations in predicting and preventing violent behavior contributes to this illusion of control. There is an urgent need for people to feel more in control of their lives that outweighs reason. When violence occurs, it is natural to feel threatened, anxious, and unsafe. Feeling unsafe comes from an individual perceiving that they have less control over their own physical security and over their future. So, while attributing violence to mental illness allows people to believe they have some control over their safety, like mandating treatment for people with mental illness, the truth is that even when people with mental illness are in treatment, there is no guarantee that they will not act violently. That people fall prey to this cognitive bias is supported by the results of the 2013 Gallup and 2022 Monmouth University polls presented in the last chapter,[53] where half the those surveyed blamed the mental health system or mental health problems for mass shootings. In fact, these polls showed that mental illness was viewed by the general public as the *top* cause of violence. If that is what people think—that mental illness is *the* primary cause of violence—then it is unsurprising that a reaction would be a desire to do something to address that cause to prevent violence.

There are three truisms about mental health treatment that can be used to counter this cognitive bias. *First, mental health experts do not have a crystal ball to predict violence.* Many people may hope that mental health clinicians can somehow accurately predict future outcomes in people's lives, including whether people will commit violence. However, over 30 years of research have shown that mental health professionals are only somewhat better than random chance at such predictions.[87] On the one hand, scientific research has developed a number of violence risk assessment instruments and tools that can improve the accuracy of predictions of violence.[88] On the other hand, these violence risk assessment tools do not claim to have perfect accuracy. Limitations exist,[89] and clinicians do not always rely on violence risk assessment tools (and thus remain vulnerable to decision-making errors[90]). Scoring of these tools might also be influenced by factors unrelated to the person being assessed—whether, for example, the administering clinician is hired by a prosecutor or by a defense attorney[91]—showing there are barriers toward implementation of risk assessment technology in real-world settings. It is critical, therefore, for the public and policymakers to know that when violence occurs, even if the perpetrator was being treated for mental illness, it is unrealistic to expect that the violence could have been foreseen and stopped by the treating clinician.

Second, mental health experts do not have a magic potion to prevent violence. Limited studies have examined the effects of antipsychotic medication on reducing violent behavior.[92] We are aware of no findings that show reduced violence with medications for bipolar or major depressive disorder. Similarly, there has been no definitive mode of psychotherapy that has shown consistent effectiveness in reducing violent behavior. If symptoms of mental illness are related to violent thoughts or behaviors, then treatment could potentially be effective. There exists no pill whose primary effect is to prevent people from being violent, including those with antisocial personality disorder. Mental health professionals can address the dynamic risk factors that increase violence,[93] such as anger and substance abuse, but there is still not enough rigorous clinical research to conclude that treatments definitively reduce violence (see Chapter 8).

Overall, clinical research has yielded mixed findings with respect to effectiveness of treatments for reducing violence itself. There is little consistent research showing that psychopathy, sexual offending, and antisocial personality disorder can be successfully treated with medications or psychosocial interventions (see Chapter 9). Overall, mental health professionals are generally better suited to provide therapeutic benefit to those who are suffering and seeking help as opposed to those who are not looking for any help and cause others to suffer.

It is vital, then, that the public and policymakers understand that when violence occurs, there is limited evidence that mental health treatments delivered by mental health providers would have stopped the violence. Clinicians do play a role in society's efforts to reduce and prevent violence: from helping patients manage aggressive thoughts and feelings to conducting court-mandated psychotherapy with domestic violence perpetrators, investigating child-abuse allegations, and alerting individuals imminently threatened by a vengeful patient. But much larger-scale, policy-level violence prevention is needed to address environment-level risk factors like poverty, homelessness, domestic abuse, and gun access. Exaggerating the ability of mental health professionals to "cure" a person of violent tendencies functions the same way as exaggerating the role of mental illness in violence. Both distract society from a thorough and effective response to violence that addresses stronger risk factors.

Third, mental health experts do not have extra-sensory perception (ESP) to read the minds of patients who intend to be violent. Television shows often exaggerate the ability of human beings, especially psychologists or experts in behavioral science, to detect when a person is lying.[94] Also, mental health professionals do not deliver psychotherapy sessions with their patients hooked up to a polygraph machine, which itself has inconclusive evidence for accuracy in lie detection.[95,96] There are assessments to help detect when a patient is feigning or malingering psychological symptoms or cognitive deficits, but none we are aware of specifically measure whether a person is lying about planning to commit homicide. Such tools simply do not exist. At best, a clinician can ask a patient if they are experiencing violent fantasies or thoughts of hurting other people. And research confirms that asking a patient about their probability of violence is helpful[97] and that patients who acknowledge violent fantasies have been shown to be more likely to be violent.[98] However, if a patient denies violent thoughts, this does not rule out that the patient is lying and intending to commit violence. Clinicians are not able to read a patient's mind to know if they harbor plans to hurt others.

"Thinking Slow" about Violence

The three cognitive biases reviewed are not the only possible ones related to perpetuating the exaggerated link between violence and mental illness. Two other cognitive biases may also come into play in the rare event that mental illness plays a role in a violent crime. First, a confirmation bias[71] occurs when a person isolates some pieces of evidence to support one's own opinion while simultaneously ignoring or minimizing other pieces of evidence that are equally valid (if not more so if they are at odds with one's own opinion). Thus, with respect to exaggerations about violence and mental illness, mental illness as a factor in violence will be overemphasized while stronger risk factors will be underemphasized, such as the perpetrator having no qualms about harming or killing another human.

Second, a hindsight bias[71] occurs when a person looks backward in time to find a reason for a violent event, for example: "If this person with mental illness had been in mental health treatment, they would not have been violent." But as we just discussed, mental health professionals do not have a crystal ball to predict violence nor a magic potion to prevent violence. And they do not have ESP to read violent patients' minds. Blaming the mental health system for violence is based on the hindsight bias but ignores at least one, if not all, of these three facts about the mental health profession.

What can be done about the cognitive biases that thwart an objective and reasoned evaluation of violent behavior? To counter the availability heuristic leading to assumptions that violence is caused by mental illness, which rests precariously on incomplete and easily accessible information, one must patiently explore specific questions. Is there a link between violence and mental illness? If there is a link, is it strong? What are the other risk factors that need to be considered? How strong is their link to violence compared to mental illness? In the next two chapters, we will review in more depth the research on mental illness and violence.

Before we do so, it is crucial to stress that the link between violence and mental illness is complicated. On the one hand, there is no scientific research conclusively demonstrating that mental illness is a leading cause of gun violence or mass shootings. On the other hand, does this mean that there is absolutely no link between mental illness and violence? Though the research shows little evidence that mental illness should be considered a leading cause of violence, it is essential to recognize that mental illness has been shown to be related to higher rates of a number of risk factors for violence, including lower education, unemployment, family instability, history of physical abuse, substance abuse, and financial problems. In fact, it is because individuals with mental illness often have higher rates of the above stressors that mental illness is mistakenly blamed as "the" cause of violence.

Safe communities, violence prevention, violence reduction, decreased stigma against people with psychiatric conditions, and humane psychiatric care all rely on a proper understanding of violence and mental illness. As we will show in the next two chapters, the link between violence and mental illness is weaker than commonly thought. A review of the existing evidence shows that mental illness has a complex association with violence that explains only a tiny part of the problem. This insight is vital for "thinking slowly" about violence and mental illness so that one considers the multiple risk factors underlying every act of violence in an objective and comprehensive way, prioritizing stronger risk factors in the process.

Additionally, recognizing that there are individual- and environment-level risk factors for violence[88] counteracts not only the fundamental attribution error but also the theater of control. Even if clinicians could predict and prevent every act of violence, their efficacy would be limited because: (1) mental illness is a relatively weak factor for violence, and (2) clinicians are not equipped to modify large-scale environmental risk factors for violence such as gun access, unsafe neighborhoods, and influence of hate groups. This insight is vital for thinking realistically about what the mental health profession can and cannot do to prevent violence and for recognizing what tasks fall under the responsibility of policymakers and law enforcement agencies.

4

Scientific Research on the Link between Violence and Mental Illness

The majority of people with mental illness do not commit violence.[18] Research has demonstrated that only about 5% of violence is attributable to diagnoses of schizophrenia, bipolar disorder, or major depression.[15-18] Repeatedly, studies have shown that most people with mental illness are not involved in extreme violence[70] or even minor physical aggression.[15,99,100] Even still, is there a link between violence and mental illness? Put differently, even if most people with mental illness are not violent, is there scientific evidence that mental illness is associated with higher risk of violence?

A quick primer on the technical components of scientific studies will help interpret the research on the link between violence and mental illness. "Internal validity" regards whether the study design permits trustworthy answers to research questions. In the case of studies on violence and mental illness, internal validity concerns the degree to which we can have confidence in the data to conclude that the status of one variable (e.g., violence versus no violence) is statistically associated with the status of another variable (e.g., mental illness versus no mental illness). Thus, for studies of violence and mental illness this will involve questions about how violence and mental illness were measured and whether they are valid tools and methods for measuring violence and mental illness. If not, then there ought to be less confidence in the data. When it comes to the link between violence and mental illness, another consideration is timeframe: can occurrence of one variable (e.g., mental illness) be said to be statistically associated with another subsequent variable (e.g., violent behavior)? This means that, ideally, the timeframe of the studies would be longitudinal, with two or more time points.

"External validity" concerns how well the research findings represent and are similar to the population of interest; to what extent can the results be generalized across various populations and settings? In other words, even if a study has perfect internal validity (e.g., measurement and time frame), the findings can still be suspect if the people who provided this measurement are a non-representative group of individuals (e.g., patients discharged from a single acute-care hospital in a single city of the United States). Thus, for the present purposes, evaluating external validity will involve questions about who provided the data on violence and mental illness and whether they are representative of the general population. If not, then findings may not be applicable in the "real world." When it comes to the link between violence and mental illness, another consideration is whether the study is representative of people with mental illness. If study participants identified as meeting criteria for "mental illness" do not reliably or appropriately represent the population of people with mental illness, then this also raises questions regarding the external validity of the study.

One last item to note is that the studies reviewed do not report on whether mental illness "causes" violence. Scholars have debated about how or whether causation can be inferred from identifying risk factors.[101-103] Instead, the studies in this chapter report on risk factors that are significantly associated with violent behavior (meaning that the variables are statistically related to violence beyond what would be expected from chance alone). As a result, it is important to recognize that the studies reviewed below on the links between mental illness and violence are limited to showing whether mental illness is correlated with violence or whether mental illness predicts future violence.

Epidemiologic Catchment Area (ECA) Survey

In 1990, medical sociologist Jeffrey Swanson and colleagues published a landmark study of violence and mental illness analyzing the Epidemiologic Catchment Area (ECA) survey.[15] In this study, mental illness was measured by the Diagnostic Interview Schedule, a structured interview designed for use by trained staff to assess mental health diagnoses in the year prior to the interview as defined by the *Diagnostic and Statistical Manual of Mental Disorders—Third Edition* (DSM-III). The authors created a dichotomous variable that included meeting DSM-III criteria for any of the following: schizophrenia, major depression, and mania or bipolar disorder. For substance abuse diagnosis, the authors correspondingly created a dichotomous variable including meeting criteria for alcohol abuse or dependence or drug abuse or dependence.

For the measure of violence, the study relied on five items:

1. Did you ever hit or throw things at your wife/husband/partner? [If so] Were you ever the one who threw things first, regardless of who started the argument? Did you hit or throw things first on more than one occasion?
2. Have you ever spanked or hit a child (yours on anyone else's) hard enough so that he or she had bruises or had to stay in bed or see a doctor?
3. Since age 18, have you been in more than one fight that came to swapping blows, other than fights with your husband/wife/partner?
4. Have you ever used a weapon like a stick, knife, or gun in a fight since you were 18?
5. Have you ever gotten into physical fights while drinking?[15(p763)]

In total, 368 of the total 10,059 respondents (3.7%) responded positively to at least one of these items for the one-year period before the ECA interview. Analyzing this data, Swanson demonstrated a number of critical findings about violence: (1) younger respondents were significantly more likely to report violence than older respondents; (2) respondents with lower socioeconomic status were more likely to report violence than respondents with higher socioeconomic status; (3) male respondents were more likely to report violence than female respondents; (4) respondents with mental illness were more likely to report violence than respondents without mental illness; and (5) respondents with substance abuse diagnoses were more likely to report violence than respondents without substance abuse diagnoses. A reminder: The findings here (and throughout the chapter) report on risk factors that are associated with violence to a level of statistical significance. They do not report that the risk factors cause violence.

A major methodological contribution of the ECA study was analyzing data representative of the US population. This means the study had excellent external validity because it generalized to the entire population. Previously, scientific studies had enrolled largely nonrepresentative samples from hospitals or clinics, which it was noted "may systematically overestimate violence among persons with schizophrenia while under-estimating violence associated with major affective disorder."[15(p769)] This was the first national scientific study on the topic of violence and mental illness and was unprecedented at the time, yielding valuable results to inform policymakers, clinicians, and the public about how mental illness and violence were linked.

Another substantive contribution of this study was showing that public fears of people with major mental illness are violent are "largely unwarranted, though not totally groundless: 12.7 percent of all those with schizophrenia in this study reported violent behavior in the past year."[15(p769)] The authors therefore note that while most people with schizophrenia in the sample (87.3%) reported no violence, it was also the case that the level of violence was higher among respondents with mental illness. Thus, the message was twofold; namely, while most people with mental illness were not violent, mental illness still increased risk *to some extent and for some types of violence.*

In this regard, and Swanson and colleagues acknowledge that a "serious problem was that the ECA data provide no adequate quantitative measure of violence. Though the items are varied and cover a wide range of behavior, they overlap considerably and are not specific in terms of severity and frequency. We did count the number of positive items, but the count gives only a rough and indiscriminate indicator of the severity and frequency of violent behavior. Logically speaking, a respondent who committed multiple acts of felonious assault (even homicide) cannot be distinguished from someone with only a single, less serious episode to report. This is hardly a trivial limitation; it prevents us from inferring the actual degree of dangerousness with respect to certain disorders."[15(p763)]

As a result, the measure of violence in this study needs to be considered carefully, meaning the study had a limitation concerning its internal validity. For example, while the item above asked if the respondent had ever taken part in a physical fight while drinking, it is not specified whether the person initiated the fight or was in a bar at the time while drinking and was involved in a fight they did not initiate. Further, in the above measurement of violence, it is unknown whether respondents used a "stick, knife, or gun" as that item did not distinguish among the three. Also, some items above may have received a positive response because the respondent was acting in self-defense, resulting from being violently victimized by someone else first; for example, if a respondent may have said "yes" to having used a knife or gun in the past year because they were protecting their house from an intruder. Most importantly, among violent acts not precisely measured were those of greatest concern in society like murder and rape. For these reasons, this study cannot be used to infer a link between mental illness and the many types of severe violent acts the public would fear most (e.g., homicide, sexual assault).

Another consideration is that the ECA study involves a single time point, called a cross-sectional study. Thus, it is not possible to say that mental illness preceded subsequent violence, which therefore limits interpretation (e.g., it cannot be inferred that schizophrenia led to a 12.7% rate of violent behavior). Taken together, the ECA Study had superb external validity given that it included a representative sample of the general population, though there are limitations on its internal validity in its measurement of violence and lack of longitudinal design.

Critically, reanalyses of the ECA data revealed that social context makes a difference in how the link between violence and mental illness is interpreted,[104] showing that neighborhood disadvantage was related to major depression. Further, residential mobility was linked to schizophrenia and major depression. Together these reanalyses indicated that the individuals with mental illness not only have lower socioeconomic status but also lower living stability, both related to violence. As a result, it is critical to consider mental illness in the context of social environment and not in a vacuum.

A person's mental illness may also serve as a proxy for social disadvantage. Another reanalysis of the ECA study investigated whether stressful life events significantly affected the association between violence and mental illness.[83] They also examined variables that were consistent with the concept of perceived social support,[105] such as support received from family and friends. The study found that stressful life events and social support were significant "moderators" of the link between violence and mental illness.[83] This meant that statistically controlling for stressful life events and impaired social support resulted in a nearly one-third (32%) reduction in associating mental illness with violence in the ECA.

This implies that studies of violence and mental illness that fail to statistically control for stressful life events and social support could incorrectly attribute one-third of the association with violence to individual-level diagnosis of mental illness rather than to environment-level social context. Sociologists Eric Silver and Brent Teasdale conclude: "Results indicate that when stressful life events and impaired social support are controlled, the association between mental disorder and violence is substantially reduced."[83(p63)] For this reason, this reanalysis was instrumental in demonstrating that research must consider environment-level variables such as social context to permit accurate interpretation of findings on the link between mental illness and violence.

MacArthur Violence Risk Assessment Study

In the 1990s, the MacArthur Violence Risk Assessment Study took the next giant step in research on violence and mental illness.[99,106] In this study, 1,136 patients with mental disorders (ages 18–40 years) provided data every ten weeks for one year after release from one of three psychiatric hospitals (each in a different state). This repeated data collection enabled longitudinal analysis of risk factors for violence, facilitating discovery of variables that predict odds of violent behavior in advance. The two goals of this study were to identify empirically supported risk factors of community violence in individuals with mental illness[30,99] and to optimize prediction of violence with a scientifically developed risk assessment tool.[106,107]

With respect to the science of violence and mental illness, a significant contribution of the MacArthur Violence Risk Assessment Study was that of advancing what can be considered the gold standard for measurement of violence in social science research. Self-reports of violence—typical in research—were supplemented by arrest records and police reports and by interviews with collateral informants who included family members, health professionals, friends, and significant others. This was largely unprecedented in research on violence and mental illness, and it showed the importance of gathering information on violence from multiple sources.[108]

Moreover, the MacArthur Violence Risk Assessment Study expanded measurement to identify targets of violence (e.g., family, friend, or stranger), to inform whether acts of "violence" were made in self-defense, and to conceptualize a number of specific types and locations of violent behaviors. Specifically, actions were operationalized as "violence" if they resulted in physical injury, involved the use of a weapon, sexual assaults, or were threats made with a weapon. In addition, these actions were not counted as violence if judged to be in self-defense.[109] Batteries not resulting in injury or involving use of weapons were operationalized as "other aggressive acts."[109]

In the MacArthur Violence Risk Assessment Study, mental illness was determined by a medical record diagnosis and through baseline data collection of participants using a reliable checklist of the *Diagnostic and Statistical Manual of Mental Disorders—Third Edition—Revised* (DSM-III-R). Both mental illnesses (schizophrenia, depression, bipolar disorder, or other psychotic disorder) and substance use disorders (alcohol or other drug abuse or dependence) were measured.

Analysis of the link between violence and mental illness[99] demonstrated a number of critical findings about violence: (1) substance abuse markedly increased violence rates among individuals with mental illness (from 18% to 31%); (2) strangers constituted only a small portion of targets (14%) of violence perpetrated by individuals of mental illness, the vast majority were family or friends (86%); and (3) the location of violence was predominantly in participants' homes or other residence (42%), with 21% occurring in the street or outdoors. The authors find that "the presence of a co-occurring substance abuse disorder to be a key factor in violence . . . the data on both targets and locations of violence clearly indicate that public fears of violence on the street by discharged patients who are strangers to them is misdirected."[99(p399–400)]

The repeated measurement of violence in a sample of people discharged from psychiatric hospitals raised essential considerations about how to interpret data from the MacArthur Violence Risk Assessment Study: "These prevalence rates may appear high. . . . Care should also be taken in making patient community comparisons. We sampled from the census tracts in which the patients resided after discharge. Many of these neighborhoods were disproportionately impoverished and had higher violent crime rates than the city as a whole."[99(p100)]

Put differently, the MacArthur Violence Risk Assessment Study has the strength of scientific rigor by including longitudinal measurement of violence from multiple sources. But the results should not be used to generalize about the general population and to infer prevalence of rates of violence that require the research design of a national epidemiological study, such as the ECA study described above. Moreover, the sample of the MacArthur Violence Risk Assessment Study was younger than the general population used in the ECA study, and younger age is closely associated with higher incidence of violence; thus, this too could have contributed to seemingly high prevalence rates. For these reasons, the MacArthur Violence Risk Assessment Study had superb internal validity in its measurement of violence and mental illness and longitudinal design; the study also had limited external validity given that it did not enroll a representative sample of people with mental illness or the general population.

Other studies from the MacArthur Violence Risk Assessment Study provided a number of critical findings on the link between violence and mental illness, particularly psychotic disorders. Another study found that having delusions upon discharge from the psychiatric hospital did not lead to higher incidence of violence in the next year compared to not having delusions upon release from the psychiatric hospital.[109]

Further, the MacArthur Violence Risk Assessment Study was reanalyzed to determine the extent to which psychotic symptoms (hallucinations or delusions) immediately preceded violent incidents among the subgroup of participants with psychotic disorders who perpetrated repeated violence.[110] It was found that among participants with psychotic disorders, psychotic symptoms immediately preceded only 12% of violent incidents. Instead, the group of participants with *exclusively* "non-psychosis-preceded" violence (80%) was larger than the group of participants with *some* "psychosis-preceded" violence (20%).[110] Taken together, these findings show that, when viewed longitudinally, psychotic symptoms were not factors for most violence perpetrated *among individuals with psychotic disorders*.

The MacArthur Violence Risk Assessment Study examined the statistical association of other risk factors with violence. They conducted what is called a "multivariable analysis," which determines the unique and independent contributions of each variable when they are all entered *together* into a single statistical model. The study found that the following risk factors had positive associations with violence to a level of statistical strength, which we discuss in more detail in the next chapter. Here they are, ranked by statistical strength of each risk factor:[30]

- Psychopathy
- Child abuse seriousness
- Frequency of prior arrests
- Father's drug use
- Psychiatric symptoms of hostility
- Prior loss of consciousness
- Anger
- Involuntary admission to psychiatric hospital
- Violent fantasies (single target focus)
- Grandiose delusions
- Drug abuse diagnosis
- Violent fantasies (escalating seriousness)

Conversely, being employed and having mental health professionals in one's social network were negatively associated with violence, meaning that individuals with these factors had lower rates of violence in the next year. Notably, mental illness (schizophrenia, bipolar disorder, and major depression) does not appear on this list, meaning that every single variable listed above this paragraph had a stronger association with violence than did mental illness.

That said, specific psychiatric symptoms—hostility and grandiose delusions—did have a significant association with violence. This suggests that acute psychiatric symptoms are linked to violence rather than a mental health diagnosis per se and that numerous other risk factors, such as psychopathy, substance abuse, anger, and past criminality, play an even more significant role in violence than mental illness. The strongest predictor of violence was psychopathy, which overlaps with antisocial personality disorder and includes characteristics such as lack of empathy, lack of remorse, blaming others, grandiosity, manipulativeness, not taking responsibility, impulsiveness, poor coping strategies, and deviant actions.

Finally, reanalysis of the MacArthur Violence Risk Assessment Study showed that neighborhood disadvantage was significantly related to violence.[80] Because of this finding, sociologist Eric Silver warns about the need to avoid the individualistic fallacy, very similar conceptually to the fundamental attribution error described in the previous chapter, stating that "the individualistic fallacy (i.e., the fallacy of assuming that individual-level outcomes can be explained exclusively in terms of individual-level characteristics) is a problem with most research on violence, and is particularly problematic in research on mental disorder and violence . . . More generally, these results suggest that researchers run the risk of perpetuating the individualistic fallacy in studies of violence by persons with mental disorders when they use individual-level risk factors as predictors, but do not control for community context."[80(p449)] As before, this reanalysis reveals a need to consider environment- and individual-level variables when understanding the risk of violence.

National Epidemiologic Survey on Alcohol and Related Conditions

About a decade later, the link between violence and mental illness was examined in the National Epidemiologic Survey on Alcohol and Related Conditions (NESARC). The NESARC was a face-to-face survey conducted by the National Institute on Alcohol Abuse and Alcoholism (NIAAA)[111,112] that enrolled a sample of participants representative of the United States adult civilian population aged 18 or older.[113] Wave 1 included 43,093 participants and spanned from 2001 to 2003. Wave 2 included 34,653 participants and spanned from 2004 to 2005. Violence was measured in the following categories:

(1) Serious/severe violence—"Use a weapon like a stick, knife, or gun in a fight?" "Hit someone so hard that you injured them or they had to see a doctor?" "Start a fire on purpose to destroy someone's property or just to see it burn?" "Force someone to have sex with you against their will?"

(2) Substance-related violence—"Get into a physical fight when or right after drinking?" and "Get into a fight when under the influence of [a] drug?"

(3) Any violence—endorsement of serious/severe violence, substance-related violence, or any of the following questions including, "Physically hurt another person in any way on purpose?" "Get into a fight that came to swapping blows with someone like a husband, wife, boyfriend, or girlfriend?" "Ever get into a lot of fights you started?"[111]

For mental illness, *Diagnostic and Statistical Manual of Mental Disorders—Fourth Edition* (DSM-IV) mental disorders were measured with the NIAAA Alcohol Use Disorder and Associated Disabilities Interview Schedule, a structured interview assessing lifetime and recent (past 12 months) diagnoses. These included bipolar disorder and major depressive disorder. It also measured substance abuse or dependence, including alcohol, marijuana, cocaine, opioids, hallucinogens, methamphetamine, and other illicit drugs. Participants were also asked whether they had been diagnosed with schizophrenia or another psychotic disorder, both lifetime and in the past 12 months. Participants were divided into the following diagnostic categories:

(1) No mental illness or substance abuse or dependence

(2) Schizophrenia/psychotic disorder only

(3) Bipolar disorder only

(4) Major depression only

(5) Substance abuse or dependence only

(6) Schizophrenia/psychotic disorder plus substance abuse or dependence

(7) Bipolar disorder plus substance abuse or dependence

(8) Major depression plus substance abuse or dependence[111]

Thus, an essential contribution of the NESARC is that it enabled longitudinal data analysis enrolling a nationally representative sample of participants, specifically allowing researchers to investigate whether mental illness (as measured in Wave 1) predicted violence over the following three years (as measured in Wave 2).

Two studies examined the two waves of the NESARC using the above measure of violence, one study examining lifetime mental illness[111] and the other study examining past year mental illness only.[112] Looking at corresponding multivariable analyses (statistical models that include many variables at once), the following results about violence and mental illness were found in both papers using the above diagnostic categories:

1) Schizophrenia/psychotic disorder only was *not* associated with any violence, severe/serious violence, or substance-related violence to a level of statistical significance.

2) Major depression only was *not* associated with any violence, severe/serious violence, or substance-related violence to a level of statistical significance.

3) Bipolar disorder only was *not* associated with severe/serious violence or substance-related violence to a level of statistical significance.

Overall, the data show similar findings for lifetime mental illness and past-year mental illness absent substance abuse or dependence: eight of these nine associations yielded equivalent results. An exception was that bipolar disorder only was associated with "any violence" for mental illness in the past year[112] but not for lifetime mental illness.[111] The two analyses[111,112] similarly showed that multiple other risk factors had statistically significant associations with violence, including:

- Younger age
- Male sex
- Lower annual income
- Parental history of physical abuse
- Parental criminal history/household history of antisocial behavior
- Substance abuse/dependence (with or without co-occurring mental illness)
- Perceives hidden threats in others
- Stressful life events (e.g., being violently victimized, unemployed, recent divorce/separation in the past year)

Both studies reveal intricacies about the link between violence and mental illness. Combining all three diagnoses (psychosis, bipolar disorder, and major depression) into a single "serious mental illness" variable, it was found that serious mental illness only in the past year had statistically significant association with any violence but did *not* have a statistically significant association with serious/severe violence.[112]

The NESARC also showed that mental illness was significantly related to multiple violence risk factors.[111] To better understand this, we present "odds ratios" (OR) to interpret the findings; for example, the study showed that people with mental illness were more likely to have experienced parental physical abuse with an OR = 3.69, meaning that individuals with mental illness were 3.69 times more likely to report parental physical abuse compared to individuals without mental illness. People with mental illness were also more likely to have witnessed parents physically fighting (OR = 2.51), had parents with a criminal history (OR = 1.73), meet criteria for substance abuse or dependence (OR = 2.33), be recently divorced (OR = 2.81), be unemployed in the past year (OR = 2.37), and report recently being victimized (OR = 2.41). People with mental illness were more economically disadvantaged compared with subjects without mental illness (OR = 0.75), meaning in this case that people with mental illness had a 25% (calculated by subtracting the OR from the number 1) higher chance of being in the group of participants with lower annual income than people without mental illness.

Analyses of the NESARC importantly found that individuals with mental illness reporting serious adverse childhood events (e.g., abuse, neglect, witnessing family violence) had higher rates of any violence than individuals with mental illness reporting no serious childhood adverse events. [112] Related, reanalysis of the NESARC showed that posttraumatic stress disorder (PTSD) was associated with elevated violent behavior but only when accompanied by increasing anger after the trauma, also called "posttraumatic anger," or by use of alcohol to self-medicate anxiety due to the trauma. [114]

In sum, individuals with mental illness were more likely to have violence risk factors than individuals without mental illness. In other words, people with mental illness were shown to be more vulnerable to past histories (e.g., physical abuse) and environmental stressors (e.g., unemployment) that elevate violence risk. At the same time, the findings show that mental illness alone was not consistently related to different types of violence and did not predict severe violence.

Taken together, the NESARC found that people with mental illness without substance abuse were *not* at higher risk of committing serious/severe violent acts (e.g., inflicting extreme physical harm, using deadly weapons, forcing sexual acts). Nevertheless, the NESARC studies show that mental illness is clearly relevant to violence risk but that its links to violence are complex, indirect, and interconnected to other important environment- and individual-level risk factors. The studies show that people with mental illness were vulnerable to childhood adverse events and socioeconomic conditions linked to risk of violence in ways that were independent of mental illness per se. [23]

Despite this contribution to the literature, the NESARC studies of violence and mental illness have limitations. Violence was measured by self-report without collateral informants or criminal records. Self-defense could be the reason a participant replied "yes" to the above violent actions. Also, like the ECA, the most severe violent acts (e.g., murder) were not specifically measured. Although the NESARC studies were able to examine severe/serious violence, it is unknown whether these acts included homicide, manslaughter, or attempted murder. As a result, a critical limitation is that interpretation of the data is restricted in that conclusions cannot be made definitively as to whether findings are associated with homicidal behavior. The measure of psychotic disorder was based on single questions and not with the structured diagnostic interview as done for bipolar and major depressive disorders. As a result, the NESARC studies had good external validity given that they included a representative sample of the general population and good internal validity because they involved a longitudinal design, but there are limitations on internal validity in their measurement of mental illness (specifically psychotic disorders) and of violence.

Longitudinal Nationwide Swedish Registry Data Studies

While the link between mental illness and violence was being analyzed in the United States, forensic psychiatrist Seena Fazel and colleagues in Europe were analyzing nationwide Swedish data registries to examine the association between mental illness and violence. These investigators examined both the link between schizophrenia and violent crime and the connection between bipolar disorder and violent crime. Specifically, the researchers analyzed data from several registries in Sweden, including the Census, Hospital Discharge Registry, and Crime Register. On top of this, they combined these data sources with Death Register and Total Population register data. This data synthesis was possible because all residents in Sweden have a unique 10-digit personal identification number linked to these registers.

Concerning schizophrenia and violent crime, Fazel and colleagues investigated nationwide data on criminal convictions and hospital admissions from 1973 to 2006.[16] Risk of violent crime in 8,003 patients after diagnosis of schizophrenia was compared to 80,025 general population controls. In this study, a diagnosis of schizophrenia was determined in the Hospital Discharge Registry. An individual had to be discharged from a psychiatric or medical hospital beginning on January 1, 1973. Additionally, they had to receive a discharge diagnosis of schizophrenia according to one of the following classification codes:

- International Classification of Diseases, Eighth Revision (ICD-8) (1973–1986; diagnostic code 295)
- International Classification of Diseases, Ninth Revision (ICD-9) (1987–1996; code 295)
- International Classification of Diseases, 10th Revision (ICD-10) (from 1997 onward; code F20), irrespective of any comorbidity.

Notably, the authors write that although schizophrenia diagnoses in the Hospital Discharge Registry showed good concordance rates based on records reviews, these diagnoses often were accompanied by other mental health diagnoses and therefore "specificity is fair at best."[16(p2017)] This means that a single Hospital Discharge Registry schizophrenia diagnosis would not do a good job ruling out mental disorders other than schizophrenia. There were no statistics on reliability associated with these diagnoses: clinicians made them. As a result, Fazel and colleagues "decided that schizophrenia had to be diagnosed on 2 separate occasions."[16(p2017)] This meant that cases included in the study needed not only to have been admitted to inpatient psychiatric hospitals but also to have been diagnosed with schizophrenia at least *twice*. The study also measured substance abuse diagnoses extracted from the Hospital Discharge Registry.

The primary outcome measure of violent crime was measured by any criminal conviction in the Crime Register. Data on all violent crime convictions beginning on January 1, 1973, were gathered on individuals 15 years or older. In this study, "violent crime" was operationalized as conviction of at least one of the following: homicide, arson, sexual offense (rape, sexual coercion, child molestation, indecent exposure, or sexual harassment), assault, illegal threats, intimidation, or robbery. Of note, the authors excluded burglary and other property offenses, traffic offenses, and drug offenses. Also, the authors note that because there is no plea bargaining in Sweden, conviction data includes not only cases in which an individual—whether diagnosed with mental illness or not—served a criminal sentence but also cases in which the prosecutor decided to caution or fine the defendant.

Diagnoses had to occur *before* the violent crimes to be included in the analysis. From these sources,[16] Fazel and colleagues found the following:

- 1054 (13.2%) of individuals with schizophrenia had at least one violent offense compared with 4276 (5.3%) of individuals without schizophrenia who served as controls in the general population (adjusted OR = 2.0). This adjusted odds ratio of 2.0 means that patients with schizophrenia were twice as likely to have a violent crime conviction compared to those in the general population without schizophrenia. By "adjusted," the authors statistically controlled for and included other variables called "covariates" in their analysis: age, sex, income, and marital and immigration status.
- The rate of violent crime was higher among individuals with co-occurring substance abuse and schizophrenia (27.6%). Risk of violent crime was higher for this group (adjusted OR = 4.4). This adjusted odds ratio of 4.4 means that individuals with schizophrenia and substance abuse were 4.4 times more likely to have violent crime convictions compared to those in the general population without schizophrenia.
- The rate of violent crime was lower in individuals with schizophrenia without co-occurring substance abuse (8.5%; adjusted OR = 1.2). This adjusted odds ratio of 1.2 means that patients with schizophrenia and without substance abuse were 1.2 times more likely to have violent crime convictions compared to those in the general population without schizophrenia.

Using the same data sources and operationalization of criminal convictions as above, Fazel and colleagues examined the association between diagnoses of bipolar disorder and violent crime.[115] Again, the authors relied on at least two separate Hospital Discharge Registry diagnoses for a case to be included in the sample as having received a discharge diagnosis of bipolar disorder. In this study, violent crime rates among 3743 individuals with two or more discharge diagnoses of bipolar disorder were compared to 37,429 general population controls. The study found:

- It was found that 314 individuals with bipolar disorder (8.4%) had been convicted of a violent crime, more than in the 1312 individuals in the general population (3.5%) (adjusted OR = 2.3).
- Violent crime was higher among individuals with bipolar disorder and co-occurring substance abuse (adjusted OR = 6.4).
- Violent crime was lower in individuals with bipolar disorder but who did not have co-occurring substance abuse (adjusted OR = 1.3).[115]

Taken together, both studies find that individuals who had received inpatient diagnoses of schizophrenia or bipolar disorder had a higher risk of being convicted for a violent crime but that this higher risk was much more pronounced in individuals who had also received inpatient diagnoses of substance abuse disorder. This is similar to findings from the MacArthur Violence Risk Assessment Study and the NESARC, which also showed that individuals with these co-occurring mental illness and substance abuse disorders had markedly higher risk.

These studies made a number of significant contributions to the scientific literature on violence and mental illness. First, no other studies have taken official nationwide registry and criminal conviction data to examine the link between violence and mental illness. Second, no other studies on the link between violence and mental illness have used decades of longitudinal data to study this association. Third, the sample sizes are substantial and by definition nationally representative, meaning the study has excellent external validity with respect to generalizing to the country's entire population and boosts confidence in the data. Fourth, the studies take steps to at least statistical control for a few demographic variables such as age, sex, income, and marital status. Fifth, unlike most studies on the topic, the researchers were able to include a measure of violence that included homicide, clearly relevant to generalizing findings to violence that is of greatest concern to public safety. Overall, these studies have made a significant advance in the field and are unprecedented.

One of the strengths of this data is the number of cases and time examined, but a limitation is that there are relatively few variables measured, especially compared to the MacArthur Violence Risk Assessment Study and the NESARC. Fazel and colleagues provide an adjusted analysis controlling for a few demographic variables, but this raises the question as to what other covariates should have been controlled for to have more confidence in the data. Recall above from the NESARC that witnessing parents physically fighting, childhood physical abuse, being recently divorced, perceiving threats, unemployment, and being recently victimized not only were higher among people with mental illness but also predicted violence. This suggests that the diagnosis of "schizophrenia" may be serving as a proxy for these violent risk factors to some extent; this cannot be ruled out given the data and limited measures collected. Recall earlier that reanalyses of the ECA and MacArthur Violence Risk Assessment Study showed that unless environment-level variables are statistically controlled for, then the link between mental illness and violence can be artificially inflated.

Additionally, there are issues of both external and internal validity with respect to measurement of mental illness. In the ECA, NESARC, and MacArthur Study, research investigators ensured the standard measurement of mental illness by trained interviewers; in the Swedish studies, there were no equivalent quality control steps taken because they relied on chart diagnoses. Chart diagnoses therefore depend on quality of training of the clinicians, which is unknown and therefore could have been poor. Chart diagnoses, too, will be less accurate if the hospital stay was shorter; for example, the diagnosis may be based on limited information if made in the context of a short two-day acute psychiatric hospitalization versus a two-month long-term care hospitalization.

Finally, it is crucial to recognize that by selecting for individuals who were hospitalized *twice* for schizophrenia or bipolar disorder, the authors were *not* including a representative group of individuals with these diagnoses. Many individuals with these diagnoses receive outpatient psychiatric care all their lives and are never hospitalized because symptoms do not become so severe as to impede functioning. Some might be hospitalized once in their lives but afterward are stable on outpatient medication and treatment. Others may receive little-to-no treatment at all. Again, these individuals, who would meet criteria for the diagnosis, would not have been included in this study as having mental illness.

For these reasons, the longitudinal analyses arguably selected a subset of individuals with schizophrenia or bipolar disorder with greater severity of symptoms compared to individuals with schizophrenia or bipolar disorder who are not hospitalized twice or even once. Thus, there are limitations generalizing the data to all individuals with schizophrenia or bipolar disorder; these findings relate to individuals with these diagnoses who had been hospitalized at least twice. Overall, the Swedish study had incredible external validity given that it included a representative sample of the general population and also outstanding internal validity because it involved a longitudinal design, but there are limitations on its internal validity in its measurement of violence and limitations on its external and internal validity because of its measurement of mental illness.

Synthesis of Literature on Violence and Mental Illness

Overall, studies show that there is an intricate link between mental illness and violence that needs to be viewed in light of study inconsistencies and limitations in both internal and external validity. The ECA study shows a direct link between mental illness and violence, whereas the MacArthur Violence Risk Assessment Study did not find this link. The NESARC and Swedish studies found that mental illness and violence were connected but that this link was substantially weakened when substance abuse was not present. Then NESARC studies failed to find a direct relationship between severe violence and mental illness without substance abuse.

How is one to understand these disparate findings? A first set of considerations concerns inconsistencies and limitations in measurement of violence (see Table 4.1). The ECA and NESARC use self-reported violence, the Swedish studies use arrest records, and the MacArthur Study uses self-reported violence, arrest records, and collateral informants. The MacArthur Study showed that self-reported violence captures more violent acts than do arrest records because only a fraction of violent acts led to criminal legal involvement. As a result, the Swedish studies miss a sizable proportion of violent acts. Conversely, self-reported violence also has limitations because there is a lower likelihood of participants reporting that they engaged in a socially undesirable behavior. The prevalence rates in the ECA and NESARC may therefore be artificially low and, consequently, inaccurate. The MacArthur Study had the most comprehensive measurement of violence of any study to date, and that study showed no link between a diagnosis of mental illness (absent substance abuse) and violence.

TABLE 4.1: Strengths and Limitations in Studies Examining the Link between Mental Illness and Violence

	Internal Validity			External Validity	
	Measurement of Mental Illness	Measurement of Violence	Study Design Timeframe	Representative of General Population	Representative of People with Mental Illness
ECA Study	Strength—researchers trained to administer reliable diagnostic interviews	Limitation—lack of arrest records and some violent acts not measured (e.g., homicide)	Limitation—cross-sectional design restricts allowing inference between mental illness and subsequent violence	Strength—sampling frame representative of the United States population	Strength—mental illness measured in national sample
MacArthur Violence Risk Assessment Study	Strength—researchers trained to administer reliable diagnostic interviews plus chart diagnoses	Strength—multiple sources including arrest records, self-report, and collateral report	Strength—longitudinal design allowing inference between mental illness and subsequent violence	Limitation—patients discharged from psychiatric facilities not representative of the general population	Limitation—patients discharged from psychiatric facilities not representative of the all people with mental illness
NESARC	Strength—researchers trained to administer reliable diagnostic interviews Limitation—measure of psychosis not based on diagnostic interview	Limitation—lack of arrest records and limitation—some violent acts not measured (e.g., homicide)	Strength—longitudinal design allowing inference between mental illness and subsequent violence	Strength—sampling frame representative of the United States population	Strength—mental illness measured in a national sample
Longitudinal Nationwide Swedish Registry Data Studies	Limitation—reliance on medical chart diagnosis with no data on reliability or training of clinicians	Strength—violence crimes registry	Strength—longitudinal design allowing inference between mental illness and subsequent violence	Strength—sample frame includes entire population of Sweden	Strength—mental illness measured in a national sample Limitation—patients with two psychiatric hospitalizations for mental illness not representative of the all people with mental illness

The second set of considerations concerns inconsistencies and limitations in study populations and measurement of mental illness. The MacArthur Study was not representative of the general population whereas the ECA, NESARC, and Swedish studies were. The ECA and NESARC use diagnostic interviews, the Swedish studies used medical records, and the MacArthur Study uses diagnostic interviews and medical records. The ECA, NESARC, and MacArthur Study considered a participant to have mental illness if they met criteria for the disorder, whereas the Swedish studies required two or more medical records from psychiatric hospitalizations confirming the condition. This means that many patients who would have qualified for mental illness, say on the ECA or NESARC, may or may not have qualified for mental illness on the Swedish studies. This also means that there was a higher bar of severity to be considered to have mental illness in the latter compared to the former studies.

The third set of considerations concerns inconsistencies and limitations in measurement of other variables called "covariates." Covariates need to be controlled for in statistical models because they can be statistically related to both the predictor and outcome. For example, poverty relates to mental illness and violence, so it should be controlled for statistically. If that is not done, the results may be inaccurate.[80,83,104] This is important because in the longitudinal Swedish studies, mental illness may be serving as a proxy for other variables (e.g., childhood abuse, unemployment) that underlie the statistical links with violence. Without controlling for these variables, it is unknown whether the relationships between mental illness and violence are genuine or due to nonmental illness factors. Methodologically, the MacArthur and NESARC studies statistically controlled for historical and social-environmental variables that could be related to mental illness and violence.

5

Scientific Research on the Strength of Violence Risk Factors

The best scientific studies on violence and mental illness still have their imperfections; thus, inferences about *whether* there is a link between violence and mental illness need to be made tentatively. But what do these studies say about *the extent of the connection* between violence and mental illness? And how does mental illness compare to other risk factors for violence?

In Chapter 4, we reported on whether statistical associations between mental illness and violence were "significant." What does that mean? To anyone who has not taken statistics, the word "significant" might be equated with "substantial," such as would be reflected in the *Webster's Dictionary* definition "of a noticeably or measurably large amount." However, *statistical* significance means something different. Specifically, statistical significance refers to the probability that an observed link between two variables is *not* due to chance or random error.

To illustrate, two hypothetical studies may find a statistically significant difference in violence rates comparing people with or without criminal history. In one study, those with criminal history may have a violence rate of 55% while those without criminal history may have a violence rate of 45%. In a second study, researchers may find a 90% violence rate for the group with criminal history versus a 10% violence rate for the other group without criminal history. Notice the second comparison looks different by a much larger percentage than the first. Nevertheless, both comparisons could qualify for statistical significance.

A crucial point in statistics is that the statistical significance is affected by a number of factors including the size of the sample and the variability of the measures. Here is the process by which p-values are calculated:

1. We first create a null hypothesis postulating that no relationship exists between two variables (e.g., we are hypothesizing that

violence and mental illness are unrelated). In other words, if our data are consistent with the null hypothesis, then the relationship found between two variables would be zero (i.e., essentially no difference in levels of violence between people with and without mental illness).

2. We next propose an alternative hypothesis; namely, that there is a relationship between two variables. A corollary is that the null hypothesis will be shown to be false; in statistical language, we will reject the null hypothesis in favor of its alternative. In other words, we hypothesize that the two variables are related to one another (e.g., violence and mental illness are statistically associated).

3. As a third step, we estimate statistical significance with a p-value that ranges from 0 to 1. Basically, a p-value measures the likelihood that a relationship between two variables occurred by chance. Two outcomes can occur:

    a. A p-value less than 0.05 is called "statistically significant." This means that the relationship between two variables found in the data is unlikely to be due to chance or random occurrence. Put differently, $p<0.5$ means that the probability of finding a relationship between two variables *just by chance* is less than 5% (or 1 time in 20). In this case, the alternative hypothesis that violence and mental illness are associated is probably true, telling us that a relationship between the two variables is likely to exist.

    b. Conversely, if the p-value is greater than 0.05, then this indicates that the relationship between two variables is not statistically significant and that the null hypothesis is likely true (i.e., violence and mental illness are not related).

Applied to the review in Chapter 4, the ECA did find a statistically significant association ($p < .05$) between violence and mental illness; nevertheless, the NESARC, Swedish Registry studies, and MacArthur Violence Risk Assessment Study noted that the association between mental illness and violence was much more substantial in the presence of co-occurring substance abuse. The NESARC and Swedish Registry studies showed this link was weaker without co-occurring substance abuse, and the MacArthur Study did not find a statistically significant link to violence absent substance abuse ($p>.05$). This implies a need to go beyond examining *whether or not* there is a link between violence and mental illness; rather, it is critical to examine *how big* is the link.

To summarize: if there is a statistically significant association between two variables (p<.05), then this means this association is likely not due to chance. But p<.05 alone does not communicate whether this association is strong or weak. For these reasons, a cardinal rule is that the level of probability (p-value) should not be used as an index of *the strength* of an association.[116]

The upshot is that p-values can only go so far, and to the extent that the general public misinterprets a "statistically significant" finding as denoting a "large amount," then researchers do a disservice if they only communicate "yes" or "no" to whether there is a link between violence and mental illness. What people also need to know is *how strong the link is* and what risk factors show the strongest links to violence.

To judge how strong the association is between violence and mental illness, we need to examine what are called "effect sizes" between two variables: "Effect sizes estimate the magnitude of effect or association between two or more variables."[117(p532)] Fazel and colleagues conducted a review of meta-analyses to report on effect sizes of the association between schizophrenia and violence and between bipolar disorder and violence.[118] Effect sizes were based on odds ratios that can be converted to Cohen's d. As a point of reference, Cohen suggested the following guidelines as an aid in interpreting effect sizes (d):

- Cohen's d of 0.80 indicates a "large effect"
- Cohen's d of 0.50 shows a "moderate effect"
- Cohen's d of 0.20 indicates a "small effect"

The researchers found what translates into Cohen's d effect size of 0.94 for schizophrenia and violence and a Cohen's d for bipolar disorder and violence of 0.78, both in the large effect size range.[118]

However, the authors noted that when conducting this meta-analysis, they did *not* account for design and methodological limitations and acknowledge that "*the overall quality of the underlying evidence was not strong.*" This means that the authors report that the effect size is large but that the research upon which this finding is based may be flawed. So, on the surface, these effect sizes seem large until you dig deeper and discover that the evidence they are based on may or may not be faulty.

Fazel and colleagues go further, acknowledging the relative lack of covariates: "Socioeconomic causes of violence will rely on ecological studies that were not included. . . . One possible explanation is that the focus of many included reviews were neuropsychiatric conditions rather than socioeconomic factors. In addition, within the former, the variation in socioeconomic factors is limited, and thus studying their effects will require more general population samples."[118(p612)] In other words, in addition to study method limitations, the effect sizes derived did not account for social environmental variables such as unemployment and lack of social support, which have been shown to be related to mental illness and to violence, but which are not statistically controlled for in this meta-analysis.[80]

A more recent meta-analysis of 24 studies[119] reports that schizophrenia with substance misuse comorbidity was associated with an $OR = 9.9$ for violence perpetration, whereas schizophrenia without substance misuse comorbidity was associated with an $OR = 3.5$. Notice that the odds ratio reduces from 9.9 to 3.5 (65% drop) by statistically controlling for a *single* variable of substance misuse. What if other variables were further statistically controlled for in the analysis? Antisocial personality disorder? Poverty? Victim of abuse? Chances are that the odds ratio would drop further. But the research suggests that the odds ratio wouldn't reach 1, which would mean there was no association with violence. As previously mentioned, there *is* a relationship between mental illness and violence but it is not as strong as perceived. One reason for this is because other factors need to be taken into account to get an accurate picture of *how strong* this link really is.

Without controlling for these other factors, definitive claims about the scientific link between mental illness and violence are problematic.[80,83,104] When the authors indicate that schizophrenia is associated with rates of violence higher than control individuals, the label "schizophrenia" is being used in conjunction with individuals who do have schizophrenia but who also are much more likely to be unemployed, live in a neighborhood of social disadvantage, and experience financial strain. The latter set of variables relates to higher rates of violence and may or may not have anything to do with mental illness. But for a reader of this study to place the "blame" on schizophrenia necessitates *not* placing the blame on these other factors. If not clarified, these findings can potentially provide a skewed view on the data to the public, who are likely to be unaware of these statistical nuances.

In this regard, the authors acknowledge "[i]nformation on other co-morbidities was limited"[119(p127)] and "other background, psychiatric, and socioeconomic factors unaccounted for in these pooled analyses can contribute to this pathway [to violence], and there is research in support of early conduct problems, adverse childhood experiences, and economic disadvantage."[119(p129)] Adverse childhood experiences, conduct problems, and economic disadvantage—occurring well before the development of schizophrenia—play a significant role in violence but were unexamined. The authors also supply general ratings of the quality of studies and found about half were good and half were fair to poor, though they indicate that there were not significant differences in results based on study quality. Nevertheless, these methodological limitations need to be taken into consideration when interpreting the odds ratios above.

To systematically account for details of study design and methodology in the scientific literature, forensic psychologists Kevin Douglas, Laura Guy, and Stephen Hart conducted a meta-analysis examining 204 published studies on the link between psychosis and violence.[120] The authors coded each study according to: (1) setting (e.g., institution or community); (2) method of measuring violence (e.g., official records, direct observation, self-report, interviews, or multiple methods); and (3) violence severity (e.g., severe acts including homicide, sexual violence, or assaults resulting in serious injury and less severe violence such as assaults not resulting in serious bodily injury).

For mental illness, this study further coded all studies according to the following criteria: (1) type of psychosis (schizophrenia, other psychotic disorders); (2) general classification of psychotic symptoms (disorganized, positive, negative, and other); and (3) specific psychotic symptoms (hallucinations, delusions, grandiosity, and paranoid ideation).

After conducting a thorough analysis of this data,[120] which included multiple steps to assure that coding met strict criteria for reliability and that studies met strict criteria for inclusion, the authors found the following:

- Analysis of effect sizes indicated that psychosis was associated with an increase in the odds of violence to a level of statistical significance ($p < .05$).
- Findings varied based on study methodology, such as sampling frame (e.g., inpatient/institutional vs. outpatient/community), measurement (e.g., type of psychotic symptoms, diagnosis of psychotic disorder versus psychotic symptoms), and comparison group (e.g., psychosis compared with different mental disorders versus psychosis compared with no disorders).
- The association between psychosis and violence differed by symptoms (e.g., positive symptoms of psychosis such as hallucinations were more strongly associated with violence than negative symptoms such as disorganization).
- Once study design, method, measurement, and sampling frame were taken into account, it was found that the average effect size of the relationship between psychosis and violence was $r = 0.12–0.16$.

What does this mean? Effect sizes can be calculated using different statistics,[121] and in this case, Douglas and colleagues used the r statistic, which refers to the correlation between two variables. Correlations can take on values between –1.0 and +1.0. Positive values mean that when one variable increases, the second variable also increases. Negative values mean the opposite: when one variable increases, the second variable decreases. A value of 1.0 means that a change in one variable is mirrored exactly by the same change in the second variable; a value of –1.0 means that a change in one variable is mirrored by an exact change in the second variable in the opposite direction. A correlation of zero means that no association exists between the variables; knowledge of the change in one variable provides no information about change in the second variable. According to Cohen (1988, 1992), the following are used as guides:[122]

- An r statistic of 0.5 indicates a "large effect."
- An r statistic of 0.3 shows a "moderate effect."
- An r statistic of 0.1 indicates a "small effect."

Thus, as applied to the meta-analysis on the link between psychosis and violence,[123] the researchers found that the association was statistically significant (p < .05, meaning the correlation was probably not due to chance) but yielded a small effect size (r = 0.12–0.16). Put differently, there is a link between psychosis and violence but the average effect size of this link is small.

The authors conclude, "The findings of our meta-analysis provided strong support for the view that psychosis and violence are associated with one another, albeit with a small overall effect size."[120(p692)] At the same time, like the previous meta-analyses, this one similarly acknowledges not being able to control for covariates such as socioeconomic status and employment.[120] Nevertheless, taking all these studies together, it is apparent that study limitations are critical when determining the effect size between mental illness and violence. This seems to account for the mixed findings to some extent.

Taken together, the differing findings from meta-analyses fail to show a consistently strong link between violence and mental illness. In the case of the final comprehensive review that accounted for study methodology across 200-plus studies, the effect size between violence and mental illness—in this case psychotic disorders—was small.

Does the Link between Violence and Mental Illness Depend on Other Factors?

One reason the link between mental illness and violence is weaker than people think is that mental illness co-occurs with variables that themselves are related to violence. Put differently, mental illness does not exist in a vacuum: even when present, it is impossible to isolate it and determine it is the *only* risk factor responsible for a person committing a violent act. Still, although there was variability on the association between *diagnosis* and violence, it was shown that certain psychiatric *symptoms*—such as grandiose delusions—were related to violence. As a result, at least part of the link between mental illness and violence can be said to result from aspects of the mental illness itself.

At the same time, research indicated that part of the link between mental illness and violence does *not* necessarily result from aspects of the mental illness itself. As mentioned in the previous chapter, the NESARC revealed that mental illness was significantly associated with elevated risk of violence: parental criminal history, witnessing parents physically fighting, parental physical abuse, being unemployed, being recently divorced, having lower income, and being recently victimized. This implies that the variable "mental illness" in a statistical analysis will, to some extent, serve as a *proxy* for the presence of other risk factors related to violence to some extent—therefore it is critical to statistically control for socioeconomic and historical variables in scientific research in this area of scholarship.[80,83,104] Because a person with mental illness is more susceptible to these risk factors for violence, the link between violence and mental illness will invariably depend on the presence of other risk factors. It is difficult, then, to envision how mental illness alone would be the singular cause of violence in a person who suffers from it.

To illustrate, one consistent finding from the research above was that mental illness combined with substance abuse markedly increased risk of violence. This is important because substance abuse is: (1) higher among people with mental illness; and (2) a significant predictor of violence. Interestingly, the reasons behind the link between substance abuse and violence are varied. For example, it could be that a person uses drugs or alcohol to self-medicate psychiatric symptoms, which in turn elevates violence risk; or a person uses drugs or alcohol and becomes disinhibited while under the influence or agitated when withdrawing, which in turn elevates violence risk. Regardless, co-occurring mental illness and substance abuse raise violence risk above and beyond either of these factors considered alone.

Further, as shown above, although people with mental illness may at times be violent, the violence is not necessarily only, or even primarily, due to mental illness[109] because studies indicate that psychotic symptoms (delusions, hallucinations, etc.) in people with psychotic disorders rarely precede perpetration of violence.[110] This research explains one reason why the insanity defense is not often successful: mental illness rarely, if ever, is the sole cause of violence.

But then what are the most robust risk factors for violence? Every act of violence involves an action in which one person inflicts upon, or threatens, bodily harm toward another person. The science above used composite variables to denote whether the participant engaged in *any* type of violence. Nevertheless, there are many specific ways violence is manifest: intimate partner violence, campus rape, targeted school violence, child abuse, mass shootings, sex offenses, and so on. How does mental illness compare to other risk factors when examining specific types of violence?

Domestic Violence

Across the globe, about one of six homicides are committed by a current or former intimate partner.[124] The US Department of Justice reports that from 2016 to 2020, there were approximately 500,000 victims of domestic violence each year.[125] Such facts should alert us to the actuality that our public perceptions are skewed. The media gives far more attention to more sensational mass shootings even though domestic violence is more prevalent.

International figures show a remarkable difference with respect to being a victim of intimate partner homicide—the proportion of female homicides (38.6%) is much higher than for male homicides (6.3%).[124] In the United States, the rate is even higher: The Centers for Disease Control and Prevention found that over half (55%) of homicides perpetrated against women in the United States involved an intimate partner.[126] Though women are at times violent, men commit the bulk of violent crimes. The United Nations 2019 Global Study on Homicide indicates: "About 90 per cent of all homicides recorded worldwide were committed by male perpetrators" and "The vast majority of women and girls are killed by intimate partners or other family members."[127]

As noted, men commit the large majority of those crimes, but that aspect of domestic violence rarely makes the headlines in news media. Further, domestic violence and mass violence overlap, noted by Rachel Louise Snyder in her book *No Visible Bruises*:

> Consider, for example, Adam Lanza of Newtown, Connecticut, who began his killing spree at home with his mother before making his way to Sandy Hook Elementary School. Devin Patrick Kelley tied his wife to their bed with handcuff and rope before driving to the First Baptist Church of Sutherland Springs, Texas. You can go further back to what is widely considered to be the United States' first mass shooting—when in August of 1966 Charles Whitman opened fire on students at the University of Texas at Austin and killed sixteen people. What many people have forgotten is that his rampage began the night before, with his wife and his mother. . . . Omar Mateen, who killed 49 people at the Orlando Pulse nightclub in

June of 2016, had strangled [not fatally] his first wife—an act that is a felony in the state of Florida, where he lived, and could have put him behind bars for a decade according to federal law. Yet he was never charged.[128(p7-8)]

In the 2019 United States Secret Service (USSS) report on *Mass Attacks in Public Places*, 35% of the perpetrators had a history of domestic violence.[129] In one study, firearm use was shown to increase risk of multiple victims with respect to domestic homicides.[130] Research indicates that the "majority of mass shootings are associated with domestic violence."[131(p35)]

Many people have suggested that owning a gun, or living in a household that owns guns, will make them safer. While there are specific situations, such as when a woman is being stalked by a violent estranged boyfriend or husband, where owning a gun makes sense, overall, the data do not support that gun ownership increases safety: women still suffer disproportionately with respect to domestic violence when living in conflicted households with firearms.

Researchers studied the relationship between gun ownership and homicide across all 50 states in the years 1990 through 2016 and found that the rates of domestic homicide victimization rose as the rate of household gun ownership rose: "States in the top quartile of firearm ownership had a 64.6% (p < 0.001) higher incidence rate of domestic firearm homicide than states in the lowest quartile."[132(p311)] But this incidence rate of being victimized by domestic homicide showed that the vast majority of victims were female: "However, female victims comprised a disproportionate number of all victims of intimate partner homicide (mean = 72.9%, SD = 5.8) and intimate partner homicides by firearm (mean = 72.2%, SD = 6.6)."[132(p313)] Taken together, firearm ownership rates disproportionally affected the chances a female victim would be killed in the context of intimate partner homicide.

In a meta-analysis that statistically combined data from multiple studies examining risk factors for male perpetration of intimate partner homicide,[82] several themes emerged (see Figure 5.1). First, weapons played a prominent role in homicide: direct access to guns and the victim being threatened with a gun were the strongest risk factors. Both yielded "very large" effect sizes, which distinguishes these as some of the most robust risk factors across all of the forms of violence reviewed (either in the previous chapter or later in this chapter). Second, the perpetrator had

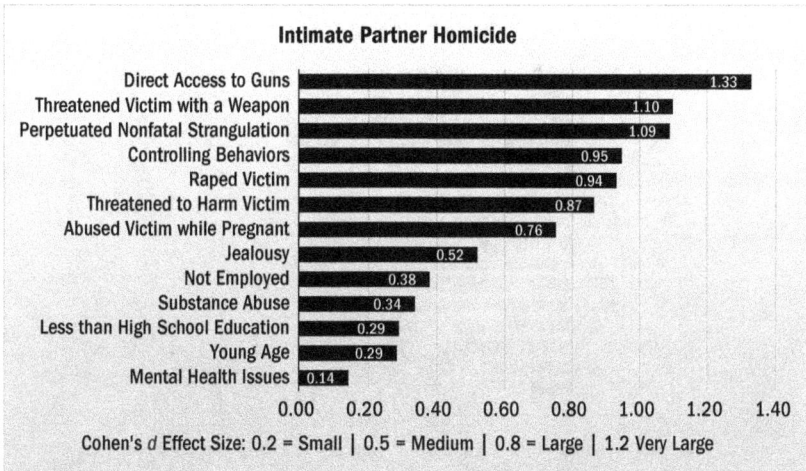

Figure 5.1: Ranking of Risk Factors for Intimate Partner Homicide[82]

already engaged in multiple violent and antisocial behaviors against the victim before the homicide, suggesting an escalation in behaviors often seen on the pathway to severe violence.[133] Third, demographics had effect sizes in the small-to-medium range, with younger age, unemployment, and not having a high school education contributing to risk of IPV homicide. Fourth, psychological problems were relevant, although relatively weak compared to other risk factors, with substance abuse showing a small-to-medium effect size. Fifth, "mental health issues" showed a small effect size and ranked lowest.

In terms of any domestic violence (not just homicide but also physical and sexual assault), a meta-analysis[134] depicted in Figure 5.2 shows large effect sizes for emotional abuse and rape/forced sex, medium-to-large effect sizes for illicit drug use and attitudes that condone violence, medium effect sizes for anger/hostility, career/life stress, alcohol use, history of partner abuse, and depression. Of note, traditional male sex-role ideology, defined in the article as having traditional attitudes about women's gender roles, showed a medium effect size in its association with domestic violence, ranked number 6 of the 16 factors below. Please note the negative sign for marital satisfaction (d = -0.63), which means that greater marital satisfaction had a medium effect size in its association with *less* intimate partner violence. Correspondingly, the figure shows that higher

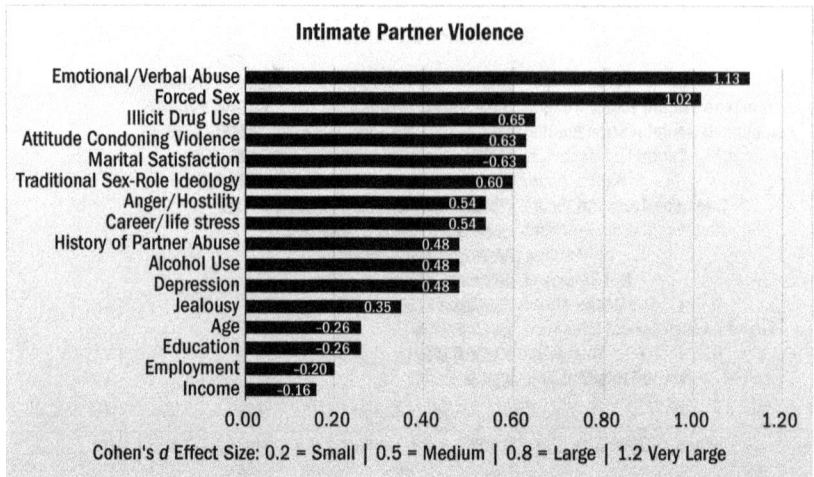

Figure 5.2: Ranking of Risk Factors for Intimate Partner Violence[134]

age, education, employment, and income had small effect sizes for reduced risk of domestic violence.

Sexual Violence

According to the National Intimate Partner and Sexual Violence Survey,
21.3% of women in the United States reported being a victim of rape at
least once in their lives.[135] In a review of 82 studies identifying factors
most strongly related to recidivism among both adult and adolescent sex
offenders (see Figure 5.3), authors found that sexual violence was best
predicted by deviant sexual preferences and antisocial orientation.[136]
With respect to the former, sexual preoccupations combined with deviant sexual interests had the strongest association with sexual offenses.
With respect to the latter, psychopathy and antisocial personality disorder had the most robust relationships with sexual violence. Employment
instability and intimacy deficits—both part of one's working and social
environment—were associated and had small effect sizes with respect
to sexual violence. There were a few other factors that had relatively
insignificant relationships with sexual violence and sex offenses, including adverse childhood environment and hostility. General psychological
problems had almost no association with sexual violence.

Stalking

In a study of prevalence of stalking in the United States,[137] researchers found that 4.5% of adults reported having been stalked, though victims were significantly much more likely to be women (7%) than men (2%). Review of risk factors associated with stalking-related violence (see Figure 5.4) did not reveal strong predictors.[138] A prior intimate relationship with the person being stalked was found to be the strongest factor. Though people tend to be much more worried about being stalked by strangers than by people they know, data from the FBI shows that people are more likely to suffer violence from known than unknown perpetrators. And homicides are more likely to be committed by intimate partners than by strangers.

The next two factors related to stalking—history of violence and past threats—are somewhat more useful. It would seem that these two variables, combined with substance abuse history, might be helpful for alerting someone whether a person they had a prior intimate relationship with might stalk them in the future. Add criminal history and personality disorders, and you have the main predictors of stalking in this meta-analysis.

But notice in Figure 5.4 that it is the *absence* of psychotic disorders that predicted stalking. A 2004 article notes, "Psychotic stalkers, many of whom have erotomanic delusions [the unfounded belief that the stalked is in love with the stalker], may pose less risk of violence because they are more likely to be romantically motivated rather than seeking

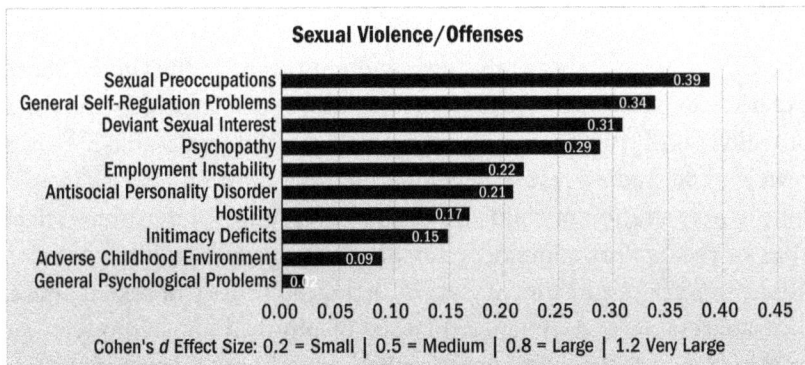

Figure 5.3: Ranking of Risk Factors for Sexual Violence/Offenses[136]

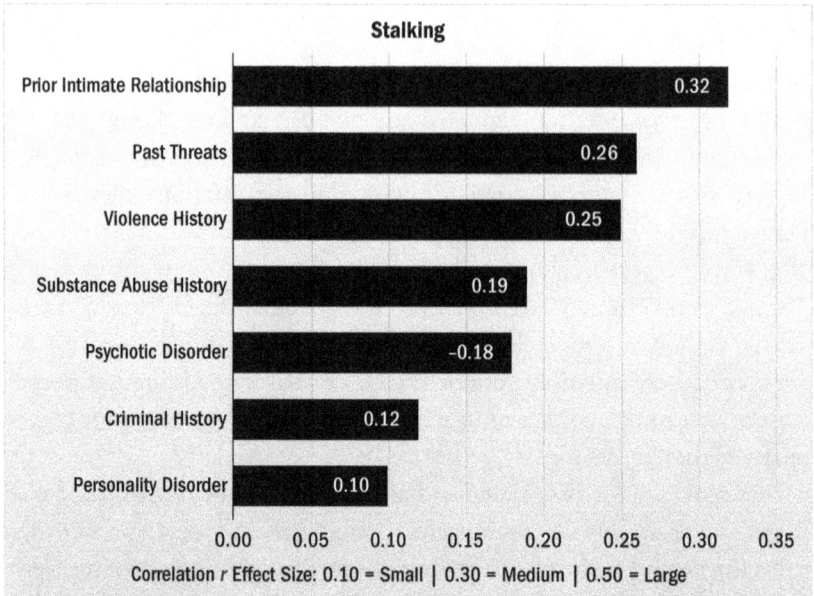

Figure 5.4: Ranking of Risk Factors for Stalking[138]

revenge."[138(p32)] This finding affirms the importance of not automatically blaming mental illness for violence. By understanding how mental illness might or might not be related to violence, one can see that there is little evidence that stalking-related behavior is related (strongly or weakly) to psychotic disorders.

Child Sexual Abuse

The CDC reports, "About 1 in 4 girls and 1 in 13 boys in the United States experience child sexual abuse. Someone known and trusted by the child or child's family members, perpetrates 91% of child sexual abuse."[139] In a review of 89 studies, researchers identified the most salient risk factors for the perpetration of child sexual abuse.[140] Figure 5.5 illustrates effect sizes of risk factors comparing sex offenders against children to non-offenders. Various historical factors, including history of sexual abuse, past aggression and violence, history of physical abuse, nonviolent criminality, and family dysfunction had a medium-to-large effect size for predicting child sexual abuse. Correspondingly, three personality characteristics were also relevant: low self-esteem, having an external locus of control (where someone attributes cause not to themselves but to outside forces), and lifestyle instability and impulsivity. The latter showed from a large to a very large effect size with respect to child sexual abuse. Several clinical variables had small-to-medium effect sizes in predicting child sexual abuse, including paranoia, depression, substance abuse, anger, and hostility, with the smallest being anxiety.

Targeted School Violence

Although they dominate headlines, targeted school violence and mass shootings are relatively less common than the types of violence just reviewed. As a result, fewer studies will be able to calculate reliable effect sizes for rarer yet highly publicized violence. One systematic approach that has been taken is to to apply strict criteria for a type of violence across specific time frames and report the *percentage* of perpetrators with specific characteristics.

In the wake of two mass shootings leading to the loss of 27 students and staff members (February 2018 attack at Marjory Stoneman Douglas High School in Parkland, Florida, and May 2018 attack at Santa Fe High School in Santa Fe, Texas), the National Threat Assessment Center

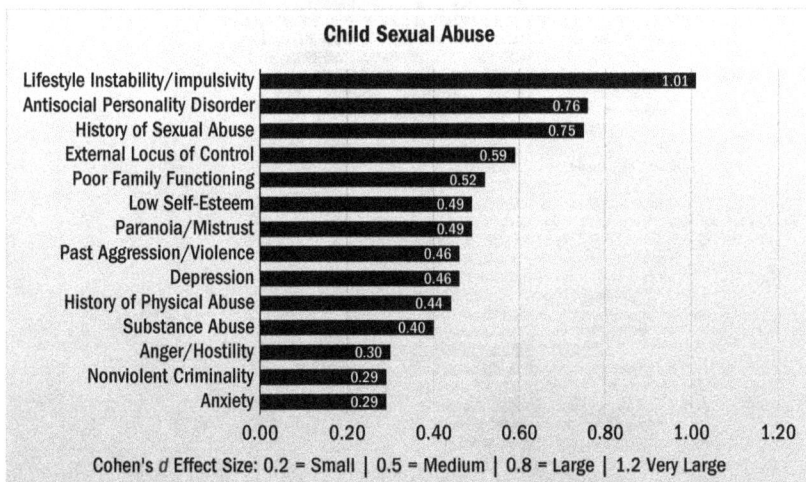

Figure 5.5: Ranking of Risk Factors for Child Sexual Abuse[140]

(NTAC) at the United States Secret Service (USSS) identified and investigated 41 incidents between January 2008 and December 2017 meeting criteria for targeted school violence.[141]

This report found that most of the attackers were male (83%) and ranged from grades seven to 12, most current students at the schools in which they perpetrated the violence. Motives varied. Most common were grievances the attacker felt toward eventual victims, who were peers and, less commonly, staff. A total of 83% of the attackers had a grievance as either their primary or secondary motive for violence. Suicidal thoughts were a motive in 41% of the cases. Psychotic symptoms as a motive for targeted school violence were rare—found in five out of the 41 perpetrators (12% of cases).

A number of characteristics were found among the perpetrators of school violence (see Figure 5.6). Overall, social stressors were prominent in the lives of every single one of the attackers, followed by academic and

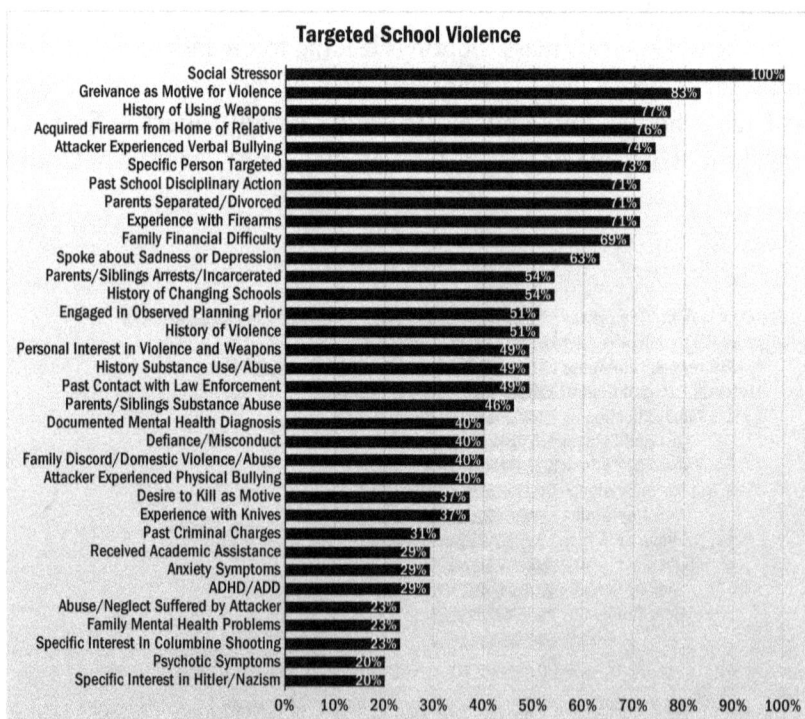

Targeted School Violence

Risk Factor	Percentage
Social Stressor	100%
Greivance as Motive for Violence	83%
History of Using Weapons	77%
Acquired Firearm from Home of Relative	76%
Attacker Experienced Verbal Bullying	74%
Specific Person Targeted	73%
Past School Disciplinary Action	71%
Parents Separated/Divorced	71%
Experience with Firearms	71%
Family Financial Difficulty	69%
Spoke about Sadness or Depression	63%
Parents/Siblings Arrests/Incarcerated	54%
History of Changing Schools	54%
Engaged in Observed Planning Prior	51%
History of Violence	51%
Personal Interest in Violence and Weapons	49%
History Substance Use/Abuse	49%
Past Contact with Law Enforcement	49%
Parents/Siblings Substance Abuse	46%
Documented Mental Health Diagnosis	40%
Defiance/Misconduct	40%
Family Discord/Domestic Violence/Abuse	40%
Attacker Experienced Physical Bullying	40%
Desire to Kill as Motive	37%
Experience with Knives	37%
Past Criminal Charges	31%
Received Academic Assistance	29%
Anxiety Symptoms	29%
ADHD/ADD	29%
Abuse/Neglect Suffered by Attacker	23%
Family Mental Health Problems	23%
Specific Interest in Columbine Shooting	23%
Psychotic Symptoms	20%
Specific Interest in Hitler/Nazism	20%

Figure 5.6: Ranking of Risk Factors in Targeted School Violence[141]

disciplinary stressors. Forty percent had histories of defiance or misconduct. Half of the attackers had recently changed schools. Half also had
recently experienced bullying or a breakup at school. Eighty percent of
attackers had been bullied by classmates.

The stressors did not occur only at school. Family factors played a key
role as well, including 71% of attackers having had parents separated or divorced, 69% having family financial difficulty, and 54% having parents and/
or siblings who had been arrested or incarcerated. In other words, the violence did not occur in a vacuum but rather in the context of the attackers experiencing multiple home life stressors—3.4 home life stressors on average.

Regarding mental health, 63% had depressive symptoms, 29% reported
anxiety symptoms, and 20% reported psychotic symptoms. Notice that
these are symptoms and not diagnoses and can stem from those situational stressors mentioned above. 40% of the perpetrators have been
previously diagnosed with a mental health disorder, which recall covers
a broader range of diagnoses than mental illness. Twenty-nine percent
had ADD or ADHD. Half of the attackers had a history of substance use.

More frequent than either mental health or substance abuse was interest in violence: 77% of the attackers had a history of using weapons
before the attack, 51% had a history of violence, 49% had an unusual
or concerning interest in violence or weapons. Furthermore, 23% had
specific interest in the 1999 attack on Columbine High School. One-fifth
(20%) had a specific interest in Hitler or Nazism "revealed through a
pattern of behavior, including attackers who turned in school assign-
ments describing their admiration for Hitler, collected Nazi propaganda
and Hitler speeches, used known Nazi references and symbols, viewed
neo-Nazi websites, wrote about Hitler or Nazism in journals, or had
conversations with classmates about these topics."[141(p29)]

Campus Violence

In the wake of the Virginia Tech mass shooting in 2007 leaving 32 dead,
the USSS analyzed 272 incidents of targeted violence on college cam-
puses.[142] With respect to factors that motivated or triggered the attacks
(see Figure 5.7), the most common was that the perpetrator had been
intimately related to the victim in 33.9% of cases. And in 13.7% of cases
the campus violence occurred in retaliation for specific actions. In 1

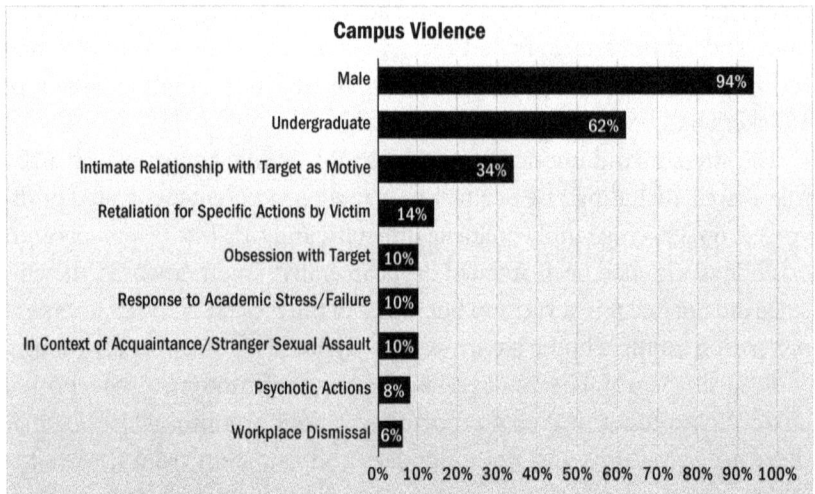

Figure 5.7: Ranking of Risk Factors in Campus Violence[142]

in 10 cases campus violence occurred due to a response to academic stress or failure, and the same proportion was due to refused advances or obsession with the target. Campus violence triggered by psychotic symptoms only occurred in 7.2% of the incidents reviewed; by contrast, the report indicates, "Handguns and other weapons were used in about half of the campus murders, which mirrored the rate of murders involving handguns in the general community."[142(p5)]

With respect to pre-incident behaviors, in nearly one-third of incidents, would-be perpetrators engaged in one or more threats toward the eventual victim. Specifically, verbal and written threats occurred 13% of the time, while stalking or harassing behavior occurred 19% of the time. In 10% of the cases, the offenders had engaged in physically aggressive acts toward the targets. The average age was 28 years, though the median was 23 years of age with a range from 17 to 62 years. Sixty percent were current or former students at the campus, while 62% were undergraduates. Most perpetrators were male, at 94%.

Attacks against Government Officials/Facilities

In a study exploring 43 attacks directed against US federal government buildings and officials between 2001 and 2013 (see Figure 5.8), the USSS identified a number of offender characteristics associated with the attacks.[143] The most common factor among the offenders were stressful negative events, experienced in 92% of the cases reviewed. In fact, more than two-thirds of the offenders had experienced at least one stressor within six months of perpetrating the violence. The report indicates that these are stressors involving family, romantic relationships, criminal charges, employment, civil court actions, education, and physical health.

Most of the offenders had a previous history of criminal legal involvement. Eighty-seven percent had contact with the judicial system, and 74% had contact with law enforcement prior to the attacks. Sixty-two percent had a history of criminal charges or arrests, while a little over half the attackers (51%) had histories of acting violently against other people. Twenty-one percent had previously stalked or harassed others.

While half of the offenders in this sample were found to have experienced some symptoms of mental illness, such as paranoia or depression, "just over one-quarter of the individuals had received or claimed to have received a formal diagnosis of mental illness prior to their attacks (n = 11, 28%), including schizophrenia, major depressive disorder,

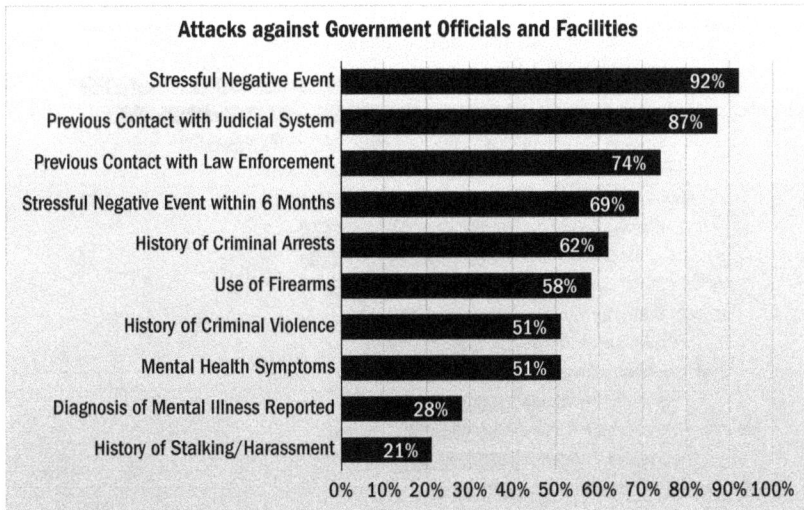

Attacks against Government Officials and Facilities

Risk Factor	Percentage
Stressful Negative Event	92%
Previous Contact with Judicial System	87%
Previous Contact with Law Enforcement	74%
Stressful Negative Event within 6 Months	69%
History of Criminal Arrests	62%
Use of Firearms	58%
History of Criminal Violence	51%
Mental Health Symptoms	51%
Diagnosis of Mental Illness Reported	28%
History of Stalking/Harassment	21%

Figure 5.8: Ranking of Risk Factors in Attacks against Government Officials and Facilities[143]

and bipolar disorder."[143(p44)] Demographically, most of the attackers were male, at 87%. Over two-thirds of the attackers had behaviors that caused others to be concerned about the risks.

Mass Attacks in Public Spaces

The USSS reviewed 34 incidents of mass attacks, defined as violent acts in which three or more persons were harmed, that were carried out in public spaces within the United States, and that occurred between January and December 2019 (see Figure 5.9).[144] These mass attacks led to 108 deaths and 178 injuries in schools, workplaces, and other public areas.

Overall, most attackers were male, nearly all had recent environmental stressors, with more than half experiencing some type of financial instability. Of the mass attacks, 71% involved use of one or more firearms, including handguns, rifles, and a shotgun. One-third were motivated by a grievance linked to a domestic or work situation. In terms of background, half had a history of criminal charges, and a little under half had a history of illegal drug use, mental health symptoms, and a history of violence. Twenty percent had obsessive preoccupations or fixations,

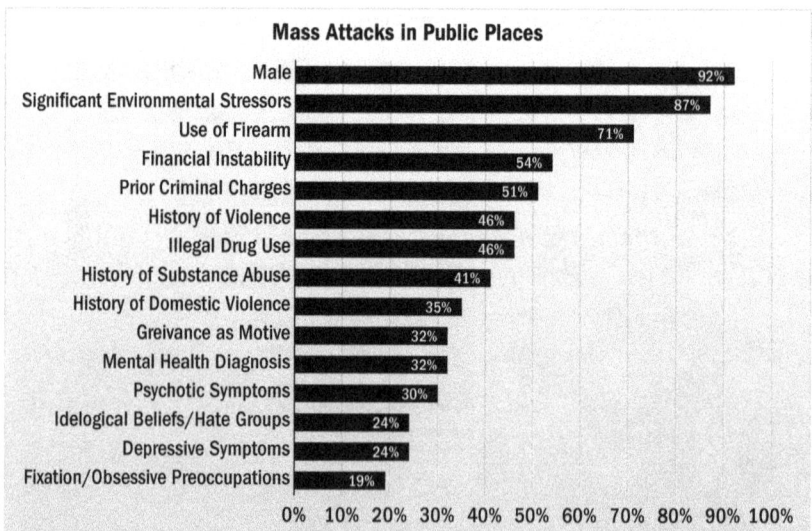

Mass Attacks in Public Places

Risk Factor	Percentage
Male	92%
Significant Environmental Stressors	87%
Use of Firearm	71%
Financial Instability	54%
Prior Criminal Charges	51%
History of Violence	46%
Illegal Drug Use	46%
History of Substance Abuse	41%
History of Domestic Violence	35%
Greivance as Motive	32%
Mental Health Diagnosis	32%
Psychotic Symptoms	30%
Idelogical Beliefs/Hate Groups	24%
Depressive Symptoms	24%
Fixation/Obsessive Preoccupations	19%

Figure 5.9: Ranking of Risk Factors for Mass Attacks in Public Spaces[144]

and under one-third had either depressive or psychotic symptoms. A little more than one-third had a history of substance abuse (41%) or domestic violence (35%). Finally, the report also indicated that "one-quarter (n = 9, 24%) of attackers held ideological beliefs, some of which were hate-focused and associated with violence. These beliefs were often multifaceted and covered a range of issues, including anti-Semitism, white supremacy, Nazism, xenophobia, antifascism, jihadism, and anti-immigration."[144(p19)] As such, groups that either explicitly or implicitly encouraged hatred and violence were also shown to have influenced a number of the perpetrators of mass attacks.

How Mental Illness Ranks Compared to Other Violence Risk Factors

As we consider the findings from these numerous studies, it is important to note that "mental illness" as a category—definitively meeting criteria for DSM diagnoses of schizophrenia, bipolar disorder, and major depression—was not listed under *any* of the different types of violence reviewed. That said, there were different terms used throughout the research to refer to mental health problems in general. This is how they ranked:

- For intimate partner homicide, "mental health issues" was the lowest-ranked risk factor (ranked number 13 out of 13). The effect size between "mental health issues" and intimate partner homicide was small.
- For domestic violence, "depression" was ranked number 11 out of 16 risk factors. The effect size between "depression" and domestic violence was medium.
- For sexual violence/offenses, "general psychological problems" was the lowest- ranked risk factor (ranked number 10 out of 10). The effect size between "general psychological problems" and sexual violence/offenses was small.
- For targeted school violence, "documented mental health diagnosis" ranked 20th out of 34 risk factors while "psychotic symptoms" ranked number 33 out of 34 risk factors.
- For campus violence, "psychotic actions" ranked number 8 out of 9 risk factors.

- For attacks against government officials and facilities, "mental health symptoms" ranked number 9 out of 11 risk factors, and "diagnosis of mental illness reported" ranked number 10 out of 11 risk factors.
- For mass shootings in public places, "mental health diagnosis" ranked number 10 out of 14 risk factors, "depressive symptoms" ranked number 12 out of 14 risk factors, and "psychotic symptoms" ranked number 11 out of 14 risk factors.
- For child sexual abuse, "depression" ranked number 9 out of 14 risk factors. The effect size between "depression" and child sexual abuse was small to medium.
- For stalking, "psychotic disorders" was ranked but found to be *negatively* related to stalking, meaning that individuals with psychotic disorders were less likely to engage in stalking behavior than individuals without psychotic disorders.

Overall, this review of risk factors shows that mental health problems are relevant to violence, but that, for every type of violence studied, they were never among the top five risk factors. Instead, mental health problems were among the lowest-ranked risk factors. There was no pattern of mental health problems showing a strong effect size; rather, for most types of violence, mental illness or mental health problems showed a small effect size, if listed at all.

As we have seen, exaggeration about the link between mental illness and violence can crowd out consideration of other more critical factors that lead to violence. Unjustifiably overweighting the role of mental illness means unjustifiably underweighting the contribution of other risk factors, such as psychopathic traits, criminal behavior, substance abuse, anger, impulsivity, trauma, child abuse, financial strain, unsafe neighborhoods, hate, gun access, criminal thinking, and other risk factors shown to have strong associations with multiple types of violence.

6

Multiple Causes of Violence and
Categorizing Three Types of Risk Factors

In their 2018 report on *Mass Attacks in Public Places*, the USSS National Threat Assessment Center (NTAC) concludes: "The violence described in this report is *not the result of a single cause or motive*. The findings emphasize, however, that we can find warning signs prior to an act of violence. While not every act of violence will be prevented, this report shows that targeted violence may be preventable, if appropriate systems are in place to identify concerning behaviors, gather information to assess the risk of violence, and utilize community resources to mitigate the risk."[129(p2)] The report makes clear that every act of violence involves multiple risk factors; there is never a single cause of the violent act.

Again, it is important to emphasize an implication of the reviews of risk factors for several types of violence outlined in the previous chapter: mental illness was only a small piece of the puzzle of violence. Mental illness was never close to being among the strongest risk factors; if it was there at all, it was usually on the low end of the list, and in some cases, it was not correlated to violence. Rather, many other factors feature much more prominently than mental illness, including situational stressors in one's family and work environments, interest in violence and guns, antisocial personality disorder/psychopathy, substance abuse, being male, being young, financial issues, and unemployment.

Society blaming mental illness for violence does not match up with the research on what leads to violence. When we hear about a violent event, instead of asking whether the person had mental illness, the research indicates that a better question would be to ask what else was going on. Even if the news media does not report on these factors, especially in the immediate aftermath of a violent event, the review thus far shows that it is critical to inquire about multiple risk factors behind the violence even if we do not have access to that information. Based on the research we have reviewed, below we propose that these "what else was going on" factors fall into three categories:

1. *External risk factors*: environment-level variables.
2. *Internal risk factors*: individual-level variables.
3. *Violence-defining risk factors*: person has the means to be violent and believes violence is an acceptable choice.

Notably, Categories 1 and 2 are factors that elevate risk of violence but may or may not be components of violence; they are not necessary for violence to occur (financial stress, for example). As a result, this cannot be a necessary part of violence. Just because someone is unemployed or has experienced trauma does not mean they will act violently. Nevertheless, the more of these external and internal risk factors a person has in their lives, the greater the statistical chances are that the person will be under circumstances that increase risk of violence.

By contrast, Category 3 involves the direct components of violence itself; namely, believing that violence is an acceptable choice, potentially encouraged by others, as well as having the means to commit violence. This is necessary for violence. Notice that the word "violence" only shows up in the description above this category. When "I'm pissed at him" (anger) transforms into "I'd like him wiped off the face of the earth" (hate), the latter contains an additional component of violence lacking in the first. Thus, this third category describes factors that both elevate risk of violence *and* define the violence perpetrated. A person can have external or internal risk factors, but for a person to perpetrate a violent act, they must, by definition, see violence as an acceptable option and have the means for violence to be a viable option. The more Category 3 factors are pertinent to a given person, the more likely that person is to view violence as a legitimate choice (e.g., if they are active in online hate groups that encourage violence, have multiple psychopathic traits, or have access to deadly weapons).

For these reasons, Categories 1 and 2 are important to understanding factors that scientifically increase violence risk but that may or may not be related to violence. Category 3 is important to understanding factors that scientifically increase violence risk and that are necessary parts of each act of violence itself.

With respect to the jigsaw puzzle metaphor, the risk factors that de-fine Category 3 are like the pieces with straight edges that are necessary for framing the boundaries of the puzzle. Categories 1 and 2 fill in the rest of the puzzle. Applied to what we will call "The 3-Category Vio-lence Model," it is vital to recognize that underlying every violent act, the perpetrator has perceived that harming others is an acceptable op-tion and behavior, and has the means of inflicting this harm. Category 3 therefore includes the factors that reinforce the message that one has the permission or even the right to be violent, and the factors that more easily enable that person to act out this violence. These risk factors de-note a willingness and ability to carry out violence and inflict physical and emotional harm on others.

External Risk Factors and Environment-Level Variables

Many of the variables we have considered stem from external factors that relate to one's outside world. First, a number of social environment variables have also been shown to relate to violence. Living in unsafe neighborhoods and perceiving threats in others in one's environment have been shown to relate to violence.[80,81,111] Inadequate social support and loss of social relationships also relate to increased risk of violence,[83] so it is unsurprising that campus violence and stalking were shown to be linked to prior relationships, sexual offenses to intimacy deficits, and the NESARC showed that recent divorce/separation predicted violence.[111] Overall, multiple domains of external factors were shown to predict vio-lence across multiple studies.

Second, history of family instability and parental criminality were prominent in the research presented above. The MacArthur Study found that the father's drug use was a predictor of violence. The NESARC showed that parental criminal history/household history of antisocial behavior predicted violence. Family dysfunction had a medium effect size in its statistical association with child sexual abuse. Correspond-ingly, 71% of perpetrators of school violence were from homes in which their parents were divorced or separated, and 54% were from homes in which their parents or siblings had been arrested or incarcerated.

Third, a number of factors regarded a perpetrator's current life cir-cumstances. Stressful events appeared as elevating violence risk in multiple studies and reviews. In particular, the NESARC showed that recent violent victimization was linked to future violence. Experiencing social stressors was ranked number 1 out of 34 risk factors for school violence and for attacks against government officials and facilities, while significant environmental stressors were found among 87% of perpetrators of mass attacks. Targeted school violence was shown to be linked to recently having moved schools. Career/life stress had a medium effect size on domestic violence in male perpetrators.

Fourth, another domain consistently related to violence was financial and work status, starting with the ECA Study, which found that respondents from lower socioeconomic status were more likely to report violence than respondents with higher socioeconomic status. This finding was corroborated in the NESARC, which found that lower annual income was related to greater odds of violence. Being unemployed was related to higher rates of intimate partner violence, specifically homicide by male perpetrators. Sexual violence was linked to employment instability. With respect to rare but horrific acts of violence, family financial difficulty was reported in 69% of cases of targeted school violence, and financial instability was reported in 54% of mass attacks in public places.

Internal Risk Factors and Individual-Level Variables

Many of the variables also stem from internal factors that relate to an individual's characteristics; for example, younger age and being male predicted violence. Other individual-level variables related to violence. First, anger and hostility elevated risk of violence according to the MacArthur Study and shown to have a medium effect size on increasing the odds of domestic violence by male perpetrators. Anger was also shown in a reanalysis of the NESARC to predict future severe violence and other aggressive acts.[23,114] Hostility was associated with both sexual violence/offenses and with child sexual abuse. Grievance as a motive for violence was ranked number 2 out of 34 risk factors for targeted school violence and was a motive for a third of mass acts of violence in public spaces occurring in the United States in 2018.

Second, substance abuse played a significant role in violence. A diagnosis of drug abuse ranked high among risk factors for violence in the MacArthur Study, while a diagnosis of alcohol or drug abuse was related to violence in the ECA and NESARC. In the Longitudinal Nationwide Swedish Registry Data study of individuals with schizophrenia,[16] the risk of violent crime was largely due to substance abuse comorbidity (odds ratio = 6.4). Substance abuse was associated with intimate partner violence by male perpetrators leading to homicide. Illicit drug use was ranked number 2 out of 16 risk factors for domestic violence by male perpetrators, while alcohol use was ranked number 10 out of 16 risk factors for domestic violence by male perpetrators. Substance abuse history also related to stalking, child sexual abuse, and mass attacks in public spaces.

Third, though mental health problems were related to violence, as we have seen, this link is not as strong as is commonly perceived. Although the MacArthur Study failed to find a relationship between mental illness absent substance abuse and violence, it did show that certain types of delusions (e.g., grandiosity) were related. The ECA did find a relationship between mental illness and violence while the NESARC and Longitudinal Nationwide Swedish Registry Data Studies found a relationship particularly when mental illness co-occurred with substance abuse. Mental illness itself did not rank among top factors for domestic violence, sexual assault, campus violence, or other targeted violence, but "mental health" problems in general were still relevant and though not ranked high, were ranked for different types of violence, nevertheless. As mentioned throughout this book, mental illness is linked to violence; however, the link is weaker than commonly presumed.

Finally, adverse events, trauma, and reactions to trauma were related to violence in the above review of risk factors. This domain overlaps with both Categories 1 and 2 as the trauma is external, but the psychological injuries from trauma are internal. Indeed, the MacArthur Violence Risk Assessment Study found that child abuse seriousness was a key predictor of adult violence, while the NESARC found that childhood physical abuse, which has an estimated global prevalence of 25%,[145] was a key predictor in adult violence. When discussing this variable in particular, it is important to note that childhood abuse increased risk of violence but did not guarantee it; most individuals reporting childhood abuse were not violent, but this variable did elevate risk compared to those who did not have this risk factor. Other studies confirm this finding, too. Adverse childhood environment was associated with sexual violence/ offenses while child sexual abuse was associated with a history of sexual and physical abuse. With respect to specific violent acts, 74% of those who perpetrated school violence had experienced verbal bullying, and 40% had experienced physical bullying. Again, just because someone experiences adverse childhood events does not mean they will engage in school violence; rather, having experienced an adverse childhood event elevates their risk compared to people who did not have as many adverse childhood events.

Violence-Defining Factors: Violence as a Viable and Acceptable Option

The external and internal risk factors above may or may not be related to an act of violence. They do not guarantee violence. A person can have a history of childhood physical abuse, parents who were incarcerated, anger management problems, and alcohol abuse but never be violent. That said, these factors certainly elevate that person's risk of violence, especially when cumulative,[146] and contribute to specific violent acts (e.g., acting impulsively while inebriated).

The third set of risk factors involve those that contribute to the belief that violence is an acceptable option and to the feasibility of a person having the means to perpetrate violence. And unlike the other two categories, we argue that this category is an essential part of every violent act. In other words, a necessary condition for violence to occur is that a person must believe that it is okay to act violently and would have the means to act violently (i.e., have the instruments, weapons, or means to hurt others).

First, psychopathy has been shown to be among the strongest predictors of violence.[147] Psychopathy is not a mental illness but encompasses intrapersonal traits (e.g., lacking empathy, lacking remorse, blaming others, grandiosity, manipulative-ness, not taking responsibility) and interpersonal traits (e.g., antisocial behaviors, anger, impulsivity, poor coping strategies, deviant actions). The MacArthur Study found that psychopathy had the largest effect size predicting violence, consistent with meta-analytic reviews indicating that psychopathy is a strong risk factor for violence across a number of populations.[147] In the previous chapter, we saw psychopathic traits feature as risk factors in various types of violence, including controlling behaviors for intimate partner homicide, attitudes condoning violence for domestic violence, defiance/

misconduct for targeted school violence, and psychopathy for sexual violence.

Second, we have seen that violence was found to be significantly related to a history of criminality and antisocial personality disorder. Past criminal charges and past school disciplinary action were ranked high as a factor in school violence. History of partner abuse predicted domestic violence, past threats and criminal history predicted stalking, and antisocial personality disorder was linked to sexual violence as well as child sexual abuse. Nearly two-thirds of those who attacked government officials and facilities had a history of criminal arrests and half specifically had a history of criminal violence. Similarly, half of those who perpetrated mass attacks in public spaces had a history of criminal charges and a history of violence. The MacArthur Violence Risk Assessment Study specifically identified frequency of prior arrests as elevating risk of future violent behavior.

Third, access to weapons and interest in weapons ranked among the top risk factors for violence. Direct access to a gun had a large effect size on homicide for intimate partner violence among male perpetrators, ranked number 1 out of 13 risk factors. History of using weapons was ranked number 3 out of 34 risk factors for targeted school violence, which also listed the following related variables: acquired firearm from the home of a relative (76%), experience with firearms (71%), personal interest in violence and weapons (49%), experience with knives (37%), and specific interest in the Columbine shooting (23%). Fifty-eight percent of perpetrators who attacked government officials or buildings had previously used firearms. Fixations and preoccupation with acting violently was also listed among risk factors for mass attacks in public spaces, campus violence, and sexual violence.

Fourth, hate groups and their ideology appear to factor into various types of violence examined. With respect to mass attacks in public places, one-fourth appeared motivated by some kind of ideological hatred toward other groups. With respect to targeted school violence, one-fifth of these attackers had an interest in Hitler/Nazism specifically. These groups specifically encourage perpetrators to believe that their violence is acceptable, which is therefore a violence-defining risk factor. Table 6.1 takes a sample selection of variables from Chapters 4 and 5 and places them into the three categories.

TABLE 6.1: Arrangement and Placement of Risk Factors in the 3-Category Violence Model

External/ Environment-Level	Internal/ Individual-Level	Violence-Defining
Lower socioeconomic status	Younger age	Psychopathy
Parental physical abuse	Male	Criminal arrests
Unsafe neighborhood	Anger	Direct access to gun
Father's drug use	Alcohol abuse	Threatened victim with gun
Parental criminal history	Drug abuse	Attitude condoning violence
Violent victimization	Mental illness	Antisocial personality disorder
Unemployment	Grandiose delusions	History of violence
Witnessed family violence	Self-regulation problems	Grievance as violence motive
Poor family functioning	Lower education level	History of using weapons
Poor social support	Hostility	Acquired firearm from relative
Social stressors	Impulsivity	Interest in violence/weapons
Bullied in school	Academic difficulties	Espouse hate group ideology
Financial instability	Perceived threats	Deviance and misconduct
Lower income level	Posttraumatic anger	Violent fantasies

Strengths and Limitations of the 3-Category Violence Model

By examining risk factors associated with different types of violence, we organized the puzzle pieces into three piles. Before reading further, return to Figures 5.1–5.9 in Chapter 5 and take a moment to categorize risk factors as external, internal, or violence-defining. Afterward, consider the following caveats.

First, the 3-Category Violence Model is intended to organize multiple risk factors for violence; it is not intended to be an all-encompassing theory for what causes violence. Rather than explain every single violent act, the intent is to provide a pragmatic tool to shift from "thinking fast" to "thinking slow" by sorting multiple risk factors into these three categories.

Second, not all puzzle pieces fit neatly into a single category. For example, drug addiction is an internal factor but can also lead to impulsivity and disinhibition, making violence a more viable option when under the influence of the drug. Youth is an individual-level, internal factor but to the extent that lack of maturity implies not considering the consequences of one's actions, being young therefore increases the chances that one views violence as a viable option (and so would fall under Category 3). Similarly, being male is an individual-level, internal factor, but to the extent a person equates masculinity with aggressiveness and violence, being male therefore increases the chances that one views violence as a viable option (and in that respect may also fall under Category 3).

Third, the 3-Category Violence Model does not excuse a person's violent behavior if they possess external and internal factors that increase the risk of violence. The third column defines the violence, meaning that this model incorporates that it is a person's belief that violence is *an acceptable option for them to choose* and they possess the means to carry out this violence. Choice and responsibility for violence are not neglected but are central to the model.

Fourth, there are some types of "violence" that are not covered by this model. These include violent acts intended for self-defense and self-preservation, controlled aggressive acts performed as part of a military combat operation, and violent acts committed when an individual meets legal criteria for insanity. The model focuses on acts of violence involving physical force intended to harm or kill someone.

Fifth, there will be exceptions to this model. There may be an individual who has very few external or internal factors but who nevertheless commits criminal and violent acts, such as an individual with psychopathic or sadistic traits. In other words, the puzzle may or may not include very many pieces from piles 1 (external factors) and 2 (internal factors). But, by definition, the puzzle will include pieces from pile 3 (violence-defining factors), increasing odds that violence is viable and is perceived as an acceptable option.

Limitations aside, the 3-Category Violence Model is consistent with other theories that categorize violence risk factors. The I³ Theory ("I-cubed theory") posits that violence is multideterminant[148-150] in that risk factors promote aggressive behavior through one or more of the following processes: instigation, impellance, and inhibition.[151,152] Instigating triggers are events/circumstances that give rise to tendencies toward physical aggression,[153] such as being provoked or rejected by another person. Impelling forces are dispositional (individual-level) and situational (environment-level) factors increasing the likelihood of an aggressive impulse in response to a trigger such as anger, financial hardship, or perceiving threats in the environment.[154] Inhibiting forces are factors increasing odds an individual will override aggressive impulses rather than acting on them. Factors that increase impulsivity, such as alcohol and drug abuse, work to reduce inhibiting forces.[155] According to I[3] Theory, violence is most likely when instigating and impelling forces are strong and inhibiting forces are not.[148] Put differently, when the strength of inhibiting forces exceeds the force of impellance and instigation, then it is more likely individuals will behave nonaggressively.

Similarly, the HCR-20 V3 is a structured violence risk assessment tool[123] that assists mental health professionals to make structured clinical judgment when evaluating an individual's risk of violence. In the chapter on case conceptualization, the HCR-20 V3 authors indicate that a decision theory of violence posits that risk factors are relevant to a person's potential violent behavior for different reasons and therefore can serve different functions. First, risk factors can be "motivators" in that they play a primary role in driving violent behavior in that violence becomes a rewarding or attractive option (e.g., mugging a person to steal money). Second, risk factors can be "disinhibitors" by reducing a person's inhibitions or other normative restraints against engaging in violence, such as when one has alcohol intoxication. Third, risk factors can be "destabilizers" and impair a person's ability to monitor and control behavior (e.g., having active symptoms of severe mental illness).

While the I[3] Theory and HCR-20v3 decision theory of violence also incidentally divide risk factors into three domains, these conceptualizations of violence risk factors are meaningfully consistent and provide support for the 3-Category Violence Model proposed in this book. First, these theories encourage examination of multiple *types* of violence risk factors and start with the assumption that there is no single causal explanation for violence: each violent act is constituted by many puzzle pieces. With respect to this book, these theories would not find that mental illness is the single factor causing a violent act. Second, I[3] Theory and HCR-20v3 recognize the role of motivation and inhibition in the decision whether to be violent, akin to the 3-Category Violence Model last category in which an individual does or does not perceive violence to be an acceptable option. Third, all three models address both individual- and environmental-level risk factors. The I³ Theory explicitly addresses situational or dispositional impelling factors, while the HCR-20v3 decision theory of violence acknowledges there may be destabilizing elements of an individual's social context that increase violence risk (e.g., unemployment). Fourth, these theories and models are grounded in science and incorporate risk factors that have shown links to violence in empirical research.

Applying the 3-Category Violence Model

On December 14, 2012, 20-year-old Adam Lanza shot and killed 20 children (six and seven years old) and six staff members at Sandy Hook Elementary School in Newtown, Connecticut.[55,156] He killed his mother, 52-year-old Nancy Lanza, beforehand, and himself afterward. The case is particularly horrifying because of the slaughter of so many children and revisiting it will be emotionally disturbing and challenging for many readers. The purpose of discussing this case here is to illustrate how the 3-Category Violence Model can be applied to sort out violence risk factors in a systematic way. What follows is a brief timeline of Adam Lanza and his upbringing.

From the beginning of his life, Adam Lanza suffered significant medical and psychological problems. At only eight days old, he had an episode of apnea, stopped breathing, and required inpatient treatment. By age two, in a special needs evaluation in New Hampshire, he exhibited significant developmental delays in speech and language skills. By age five, a neurological evaluation revealed that he never slept through the night, did not like physical affection, practiced odd repetitive behaviors, and had severe anger and temper tantrums. There were also some vague reports of early childhood seizures. Early school assessments noted issues with language, memory, and processing. Between kindergarten and first grade, the Lanzas moved from New Hampshire to Connecticut for a new position with General Electric for his father, Peter.

Adam Lanza attended Sandy Hook Elementary School, where his academic strengths in reading and math were augmented by an individual treatment plan (IEP) and occupational therapy (OT) to help his writing and speech problems from his developmental delays. Lanza's functioning improved during third and fourth grade, after which his special education needs at school ended.

Soon before Adam Lanza began fifth grade, his parents separated, and they divorced several years later. During fifth grade, Lanza and another classmate wrote and illustrated "The Big Book of Granny," a collection of stories about a violent family. The stories included images and narrative regarding child murder, cannibalism, and taxidermy. It remains unclear whether any adults were ever made aware of the book. In retrospect, this appears to be the first sign of violent antisocial personality traits in the timeline. Lanza's violent fantasies continued to intensify, so that by his seventh-grade year at St. Rose of Lima Catholic School, his teacher and principal were notably taken aback by the level of violence in his creative writing—up to ten graphic pages at a time of war and destruction. His parents' response was to abruptly withdraw him from the school and keep him at home until he reentered Newtown Middle School for eighth grade.

Adam Lanza entered eighth grade with worsening of anxiety symptoms, sleep, and appetite. During an assessment that year for severe anxiety at Danbury Hospital, the clinical team recommended that Lanza be placed in a therapeutic school for comprehensive diagnosis and treatment of his academic and emotional issues. Nancy Lanza declined the recommendation in favor of outpatient treatment for Asperger's syndrome (type of autism) and noted lack of peer relationships, inability to interact with peers, extreme anxiety, rigid thought processes, and, most ominously, a lack of empathy.

Adam Lanza reentered regular school in ninth grade at Newtown High School. His father, Peter Lanza, received a referral from his employee assistance program for Adam to be evaluated at the Yale Child Study Center. Clinicians there diagnosed him with Pervasive Developmental Disorder (PDD) and Autistic Spectrum Disorder (ASD), along with noting his symptoms of obsessive-compulsive disorder (OCD). The Yale program recommended medicine, which Adam and his mother were against his taking. He eventually tried an antidepressant, experienced unwanted side effects, and stopped.

While the Lanzas, various clinicians, and school staff over several years did their best to address Lanza's multiple problems, he was unbeknownst to them consistently participating in forums and web pages dedicated to mass shootings. And his mother was collecting an arsenal of guns and ammunition that was readily available to Lanza. By age 16, Adam Lanza was no longer receiving any mental health treatment. His educational, social, and emotional life remained uneven, isolated, and frustrating. His unrealistic goal of joining military special forces never happened. At age 20, he killed others and himself in the grotesque kind of violence he had been imagining since age 10.

Looking at Adam Lanza's case with respect to Category 1 external risk factors, Lanza's parents divorced (and his family was split), he moved schools frequently and had academic problems in school from a young age, and throughout his life had a poor social support network with few friends. With respect to Category 2 internal risk factors, Lanza was young, male, had impaired function in speech and communication, anxiety symptoms associated with OCD, anger problems and temper tantrums from a young age, and delayed interpersonal and social skills ostensibly related to autism.

A key juncture in considering violence risk factors arrives. It is important to note that many people have external and internal factors, but they do not in any way act violently. If these were the only risk factors Adam Lanza had, it is certainly possible he still could have acted violently. But his risk would have been drastically minimized without that third category of risk factors, those that not only increase violence risk but are also *necessary* for violence and increase the chances that someone believes they have the permission or even the right to act violently when they have the means to do so. With respect to Category 3 violence-defining risk factors, Lanza participated in forums and visited web pages dedicated to mass shootings; had psychopathic traits, including lacking empathy; harbored violent fantasies; demonstrated interest in, and probable obsession with, violence and guns; and had access to his mother's arsenal of guns and ammunition.

Lanza's multiple risk factors for violence can be viewed through this lens. Applying the review of research above, his strongest risk factors were that he was male, young, and antisocial, and had access to guns. His developmental delays, anxiety, and academic problems may have inadvertently served as a smokescreen for his antisocial personality traits—specifically lack of empathy and disregard for his own safety and that of others. He participated in forums and visited web pages dedicated to mass shootings. And once he had the means to commit violence, the necessary components were in place: mass shooting was seen as acceptable and rendered a viable option.

None of this review is meant to demean all the efforts of the educators and counselors who tried to help as best as they were able. Instead, the intent is to provide a case example in order to organize and think systematically about the types of risk factors that contribute to acts of violence. By engaging in this deliberative process, society would ideally consider multiple causes of violence when it occurs and ultimately prioritize methods for preventing violence that address stronger risk factors, including those that are violence-defining. Let us next take a look at the case of Brett, a young man with significant risk factors for violence whose story, unlike Adam Lanza's, ended positively.

Case Study: Brett

Brett was a 25-year-old male recently discharged from a state psychiatric hospital after treatment for schizoaffective disorder, a condition that includes a combination of mood swings and delusional thinking. Brett grew up in a large family rife with financial insecurity, academic underachievement, mental illness, heavy drinking, and exposure to violence—a blend of internal and external risk factors for violence.

He dropped out of high school, worked odd jobs, and was frequently homeless, staying temporarily in the homes of friends and family when he could. He drank alcohol or used illegal street drugs daily, his peers also had substance abuse and dependence problems and engaged in antisocial behaviors such as stealing to get money for drugs. Encouraged by his friends and under the influence of cocaine, Brett got into a bar fight, severely beat a patron into a coma, and was arrested, serving time in prison as a result.

Several months after release from prison, at the age of 21, Brett began experiencing psychiatric symptoms of paranoid ideation, which were so strong that he was eventually unable to function or care for himself. This, combined with his inability to attain a stable living, precipitated a three-month inpatient mental health hospitalization. This treatment gave Brett a chance to improve his health, separate from his peer group, and, upon discharge, move to a new city with good community mental health services. Within several weeks, Brett was living in a group home; attending a daily program for social support and vocational training, including a prep course for a general equivalency diploma (GED); and receiving regular counseling and medication management—a level of stability and quality of life he had rarely known before. His infectious smile and ready sense of humor made him a popular presence.

Yet no one ever leaves their past completely behind. After several months, one of Brett's friends with whom he had used drugs moved to town. They started spending time together, and old patterns resurfaced. Brett started drinking and using drugs again, staying out late, and getting into fights. He told counselors he was thinking about committing robberies and burglaries. His behaviors eventually affected his functioning. He became increasingly paranoid, spending much of the day sitting in a chair, vigilantly observing others. In response, Brett's treatment team implemented a plan to monitor him closely and to facilitate new social networks for him through support groups, Alcoholics Anonymous (AA), and his GED classes. The increased support and structure worked, and Brett's drinking abated, his paranoia went away, and his functioning improved without requiring readmission to the hospital. Eventually, he obtained his GED and found steady employment. He never again had criminal legal involvement.

Viewing Brett's case using the 3-Category Violence Model, he did have both Category 1 external risk factors (financial insecurity, academic underachievement, exposure to violence) and Category 2 internal risk factors (young, male, mental illness, heavy drinking). With respect to Category 3 violence-defining risk factors, Brett's case demonstrates the importance of making careful distinctions about mental illness, personality traits, substance abuse, and the influence of peer groups that encourage violence. Had Brett committed an act of violence, many may have (incorrectly) attributed it to his history of mental illness, even though his violent thoughts were active when he was abusing substances and was being encouraged to engage in antisocial behavior by his peers.

It is therefore critical to note that Brett was violent and only considered violence when he was in close contact with his peer group and using substances. The psychotic disorder was incidental to the violence; otherwise, his violent thoughts and actions were rooted in his peer culture and drug habits and not in antisocial personality disorder. He did not exhibit psychopathic traits or possess other Category 3 violence-defining risk factors.

The vignette also shows how addressing multiple risk factors can help reduce violence risk. Replacing a chaotic living environment and drug-using peer group with a stable living environment, formal education, and a sober peer group dramatically reduced the risk of violence. Had Brett continued to live in a community without comprehensive support, using illicit substances and hanging around with peers who encouraged drug use as well as criminal behavior, he would have been at greater risk of acting violently and would have eventually ended up in jail or in a state hospital. But once the multiple factors across the three categories were addressed, Brett no longer viewed violence as a viable option in his life and instead replaced it with financial, vocational, and prosocial goals.

As we mentioned in Chapter 3, mental health clinicians may not have a surefire, research-proven method of predicting patient violence, but this case shows how they do in fact help patients by addressing risk factors. They teach patients to manage anger and rage; address suicidal and homicidal thoughts and feelings; coordinate treatment with physicians, other clinicians, other professionals, and family members; treat substance abuse problems; facilitate access to services like food, housing, and financial aid; facilitate plans for safe storage of firearms and ammunition; and arrange for emergency hospitalization.

At the same time, because there are numerous environmental factors that fall outside the scope of what health professionals can do (e.g., poverty, gang membership, unsafe neighborhoods), policymakers must consistently support clinicians, teachers, counselors, law enforcement officers, and others in their individual and collective efforts to identify the three elements of the 3-Category Violence Model and their risk factors wherever they appear. And, as we detail in the next three chapters, society also must multiply those efforts by enacting strategies and policies that target and reduce proven risk factors for violence on a larger scale. This demands more than expecting mental health professionals to intervene, which means considering the myriad ways that policymakers and law enforcement agencies are tasked with addressing the three categories of violence risk factors highlighted above.

How Can Society Reduce Violent Behavior?

The 3-Category Violence Model proposed has several benefits. It draws on scientific literature to provide a scientifically informed conceptual framework for (1) asserting that there is no single cause of violence, whether mental illness or any other factor, but rather multiple risk factors; (2) systematically organizing three general categories of risk factors for violence based on existing studies; and (3) expanding on the possible pathways and interventions for reducing violence in society as informed by scientific research. The latter point is the focus of the next three chapters.

From this model, one can generate various approaches to reducing and preventing violence in society. In this chapter, the discussion moves from using risk factors to identify the many reasons a person was violent in the past to determining how best to reduce and prevent violence in the future. Society can address all three domains of the 3-Category Violence Model with practical approaches; nevertheless, it is important to review to what extent science supports these approaches. How does one evaluate the quality of this science?

Below, we provide a quick primer on evaluating the quality of research on whether an intervention is effective. First, one must consider whether an intervention has shown a reduction in violence or a reduction in the risk factor. For example, studies have shown that anger management training reduces anger. Still, fewer studies have taken it to the next level and demonstrated that anger management training reduces violence. Both outcomes are essential, as reducing the risk factor should minimize the risk of violence. But keeping both in mind while reading the science is vital to help gauge the level of scientific support for that intervention.

Another consideration is the study design. Some study designs, while legitimate, nevertheless inspire less confidence in the results due to limitations. Consider what is called a "single-armed" trial, in which, say, 100 individuals completing group mindfulness training reported lower stress after treatment than before treatment. There is a statistically significant and legitimate result. These individuals did have actual therapeutic benefits from the treatment.

But we cannot say the treatment "caused" this result because so many other statistically uncontrolled factors may be responsible for the results. What if the more severe cases dropped out and never completed treatment (or never signed up for the study in the first place)? These questions indicate the study was vulnerable to "selection bias," namely, that people with specific characteristics may have chosen (or not chosen) to be part of the study. Or, what if the content of the mindfulness training was less relevant? Was it simply meeting with a group of peers that led to an improvement? Thus, we cannot isolate the components of the intervention that "worked." Because we cannot answer these questions, we have less confidence that the intervention caused the results.

Because they are rigorous and systematic, other study designs inspire more confidence in the results due to study strengths. In particular, the "randomized controlled trial" is viewed by researchers as the gold standard for determining whether a given intervention causes specific outcomes. The 100 individuals would be randomly assigned to different study conditions in this design, perhaps by flipping a coin. Half would be assigned to an "experimental" group where they learned how to do mindfulness to manage stress, whereas the other half would be assigned to a "control" group where they were educated about stress management but not trained in mindfulness.

This study design controls subject content and group format, unlike the single-armed trial. It also controls for selection bias described above because specific characteristics of people are now equally likely in the experimental and control groups. Finally, this design allows for a critical comparison of outcomes. Suppose at the end of the study, participants in the experimental group reported greater reduction in stress than participants in the control group. Based on a randomized design, we can have more confidence that the mindfulness intervention caused reduced stress.

Of note, such randomized controlled trials lend themselves more to smaller-scale, individual-level studies than to larger-scale, environment-level studies. Although the latter can use a randomized design, as we will see in the next chapter, such efforts are not always possible as changes in law or policy apply to all constituents. In these cases, a rigorous study design would involve systematically comparing key outcomes (e.g., violent crime) between states with and without the certain laws or policies or comparing outcomes before and after certain laws or policies were implemented.

A final consideration is noting how often an intervention has been subject to experimental analysis. Suppose many different researchers have published and replicated positive results using the same methods. This of course increases confidence in the results. Methodologically, multiple studies are typically summarized in meta-analyses, a rigorous procedure for pooling results from multiple studies designed to show the strengths and weaknesses of research in that area.

When evaluating how the research supports the interventions described in the following three chapters, keep these considerations in mind. With this methodological background to facilitate evaluation of the scientific strength of published interventions aimed at violence prevention, we summarize below both the research strengths and limitations of that research, using it as a basis underpinning our suggestions for the direction and scope of future research on violence prevention.

7

Preventing Violence: Strategies for
Reducing Environment-Level Risk Factors

Improving Social Environment and Neighborhood

Violence does not happen in a vacuum but in a social context. We discussed earlier that psychologist Kurt Lewin proposed a formula to describe what underlies every human behavior: $B = f(P, E)$. This formula means that human behavior is a function of the person and their environment. The United States Centers for Disease Control and Prevention (CDC) specifically calls for violence prevention strategies to address environment-level risk factors, dividing these into relationship, societal, and community domains.[157]

A person's community and immediate social environment affects a person's risk of violence: individuals with more social stressors who live in poorer and less safe neighborhoods are at increased risk, with or without mental illness. As scholars state, "Neighborhood factors that can increase risk for violence include concentrated poverty, high population turnover rates, population density (crowded housing), and low levels of social cohesion. Low levels of social cohesion are indicative of social disorder and lack of collective efficacy, which are risk factors for violence. Physical disorder, vacant buildings, and vacant lots can influence. Mortgage foreclosures and ensuing vacancy have been associated with increased violent crimes. High density of alcohol outlets and high drug availability increase the risk of firearm homicide."[158(p254-255)]

The social environment and neighborhood significantly affected violence risk in the ECA, NESARC, and MacArthur Violence Risk Assessment Study. This consistent scientific finding shows that part of the link between mental illness and violence stems from the fact that people with mental illness are more likely to live in poorer neighborhoods and experience greater social stressors. Regarding the latter, it is noteworthy that in the USSS reports on violence, social stressors top the perpetrators' list of characteristics. Researchers note that risk factors like antisocial personality disorder, substance abuse, or acute psychiatric symptoms can lead to tense situations and that these tense situations may "turn into violent interactions because of the environment of violence/victimization in which they occur, an environment created by social disorganization and poverty."[159(p130)] Research has corroborated links between disadvantaged neighborhoods, exposure to violence, and higher incidence of violence risk factors including alcohol and drug use.[160,161]

The 3-Category Violence Model posits that violence is more likely to occur when people have external risk factors in their environment, such as when they live in poverty or unsafe neighborhoods. What can policymakers do to address this? Several experiments have shown that physical changes to what is called the "built environment" can have a dramatic impact on lowering crime. In their review "Neighborhood Interventions to Reduce Violence," social scientist Michelle Kondo and colleagues write, "Although violence interventions have traditionally targeted individuals, changes to the built environment in places where violence occurs show promise as practical, sustainable, and high-impact preventive measures . . . the most consistent evidence exists in the realm of housing and blight remediation of buildings and land. Some evidence suggests that reducing alcohol availability, improving street connectivity, and providing green housing environments can reduce violent crimes."[158(p253)] These neighborhood interventions, therefore, relate to the 3-Category Violence Model by providing a means to address the social environment with a replicable, practical approach.

In perhaps the most extensive study of its kind, a randomized trial replacing blighted vacant land with green space was conducted across an entire city.[162] The study involved randomly assigning 541 vacant lots in neighborhoods below the poverty line into either experimental or control study arms. These vacant lots themselves were randomly sampled. The authors explain that the experimental arm involved the following:

- Cleaning and greening vacant lots across the city by removing trash and debris
- Grading the land

- Planting new grass using a hydroseeding method that can quickly cover large areas of land
- Planting a small number of trees to create a parklike setting
- Installing low wooden perimeter fences
- Regularly maintaining the newly treated lot throughout the postintervention period[162(p2947)]

The authors explain further that the "fencing was a visible sign that the lot was cared for and deterred illegal dumping, but was purposely low (about 1 m high) and included multiple ungated openings to encourage entry and use of the newly greened lot by residents."[162(p2947)] According to the authors, the cost was minimal: $5 per square meter for the initial work and $0.50 per square meter for maintenance. Vacant lots in the control study arm did not receive this treatment.

The investigators measured longitudinal outcomes from police reports and sampled participants and analyzed whether there were any differences in these outcomes over a three-year study period between the experimental and control study arms. The authors reported that treatment of vacant lots was associated with reduced crime (−13.3%) and reduced gun violence (−29.1%). Also, the intervention led to more socializing in outdoor spaces (+75.7%) and to lower occurrence of burglary (−21.9%) and nuisances (−30.3%). People living near the treated vacant lots (i.e., those in the experimental study arm) perceived less crime (−36.8%) and less concern for thier safety when leaving their homes (−57.8%) compared to people not living near treated vacant lots (i.e., those in the control study arm). Notably, that intervention changed both objective violent crime and subjective perceptions of safety. That such interventions are effective and local, affordable, feasible, and beneficial to cities' overall property values makes them attractive from a policy standpoint.

Research also shows that local home improvement programs in high-crime urban areas have shown a significant reduction in crime.[163] Such scalable "place-based" environmental interventions involve repairing damaged homes, such as fixing damage to plumbing, roofing, electrical wiring, or heating. The intervention provided up to $20,000 for each homeowner to make these home improvements located in urban low-income neighborhoods (with a mean monthly income of $993). In one study, a total of 13,632 houses on 6,732 city blocks received this assistance, and researchers investigated whether it would be associated with reduced crime specifically on streets where homes had been repaired.[163] Analysis showed that structural home repairs were associated with decreased total crime, violence, and robbery. Critically, blocks in urban low-income neighborhoods that received funds for home improvements *saw a 22% decrease in homicide.*

These studies show that interventions to improve the social environment can impact violence and crime. One critical takeaway is that addressing individual-level risk factors is not enough and would still leave unaddressed environmental-level risk factors. Suppose a person excels at anger management training. If they walk home and see disrepair, lack a stable living situation, or witness violence in their neighborhoods, then the anger management training will only go so far. Suppose they return to an unsafe community, home, or family. The environmental foundation to prevent violence will be very flimsy for that person. These scalable environmental interventions are consistent with the conceptualization that risk of violence increases when there are more external risk factors in peoples' environments.

Addressing and Bolstering Financial Well-Being

Another main area to address to reduce external risk factors relates to financial well-being. Financial desperation can fuel domestic conflicts, property crimes, and violence against victims involved in both. While financial stress is less often the focus of analyses of mass violence, the USSS report in Chapter 5 showed that over two-thirds (69%) of perpetrators of targeted school violence were from financially unstable families. Financial debt and bankruptcy were associated with increased violence risk in the NESARC.[23] In a market society requiring substantial personal responsibility for managing costs associated with such areas as health care, higher education, and retirement, in addition to more day-to-day budgeting, reducing financial strain could potentially help individuals avoid the worst money woes (bankruptcy, homelessness) and manage inevitable money challenges (mortgage, credit cards). And in the process, this reduction in financial burdens could mitigate risk factors for assault, homicide, and suicide.

There have been studies looking at the effect of income interventions on violence and crime. On the one hand, mixed evidence exists that increasing someone's income will reduce the likelihood of crimes being committed by that person. Several studies show that substance-abuse-related crime increased when targeted individuals receive payments or dividend checks.[164] On the other hand, scholars indicate that large government transfers and financial aid stimulus have resulted in overall reductions in violence.[165]

In one of the more influential studies on this topic, data was collected for eight years in a representative sample of 1,420 rural children from low-income Native American families residing in western North Carolina.[166] Halfway through data collection in this study, a casino opened on an Indian Reservation. This event gave study participants' families an income supplement that increased every year. Fortuitously, this enabled researchers to study whether the income supplement was associated with better outcomes because this occurred during the middle of a study and allowed examination of how study participants and their families were doing before and after the income supplement. In other words, the researchers could statistically control for variables and therefore isolate a causal effect of the income supplement on outcomes.

Germane to this book, researchers found that in following the income supplement, children had significantly lower conduct disorders (the precursor to antisocial personality disorder), as well as lower incidence of other related childhood problems such as oppositional disorders. The authors state: "An income intervention that moved families out of poverty for reasons that cannot be ascribed to family characteristics had a major effect . . . results support a social causation explanation for conduct and oppositional disorder."[166(p2023)] Correspondingly, reviews show that "interventions similar to basic income" show "strong positive effects" across multiple studies.[164] This conclusion is consistent with a comprehensive meta-analysis showing that lower socioeconomic status is substantially associated with more significant psychopathology in children and adolescents.[167]

But can overall financial well-being be improved beyond simply providing individuals and families with more money? Do financial literacy and financial education work? If so, how? And does this translate to reduced risk of violence? Although earlier meta-analyses found that interventions to improve financials had limited effects,[168] more recent reviews have sought to identify specific aspects of financial interventions that do improve outcomes.[169] In a comprehensive overview of the literature aiming to identify successful elements of financial education, it was found that programs were effective when they adapted to the specific financial needs of the participants.[169] Many financial education programs are too broad, and so efforts need to target specific populations and critical lifespan timepoints, including with teenagers, college students, new parents, new homeowners, and prospective investors.

Additionally, it was found that financial literacy programs need to address the motivation of clients, not just provide information and education.[169] Leading scholars note that many people have difficulty following through on planned actions; consequently, education alone may not be sufficient; people need tools to change financial behaviors.[170] Thus, financial literacy must involve not just lectures but instruction on the use of tools relating to how to create a budget, open a bank account, avoid financial scams, obtain a credit report, balance a checkbook, borrow money knowledgeably, use a calendar to pay bills on time, avoid financial exploitation, and learn daily strategies to save money.

Finally, innovative use of modern technology can have beneficial effects on financial behaviors.[169] For example, researchers have noted that many people do not save enough for retirement. Based on this observation, it was hypothesized that if an individual had a greater connection between their present and future self, they would save more money. Researchers conducted four studies in which participants were randomly assigned to two groups.[171] In the experimental group, participants interacted with realistic virtual renderings of their future selves; for example, they were first shown a young version of their avatar and afterward an age-morphed version. Participants in the control condition were shown a digital avatar but did not interact with an avatar representing their future selves. The researchers found that compared to control participants, experimental participants who interacted with their future selves showed a greater tendency to "delay discount," meaning to accept later monetary rewards instead of immediate ones.

A meta-analysis verifies positive effects of numerous financial interventions on increased savings and decreased spending.[172] These included: paying cash only (not having a credit card), using a savings projection plan, writing a shopping list, setting a specific financial goal, tracking one's bank account, using a savings account with no early withdrawals versus having an early withdrawal fee, shopping with a budget, making money difficult to access, thinking about a reason for a financial goal, and imaging one's future self. With these simple financial self-control strategies, across multiple studies, the researchers found medium effect sizes (Cohen's d = 0.57) for these inexpensive and simple strategies to reduce spending and increase savings.

Such interventions leading to a person saving more money and getting out of debt would help reduce risk factors in one's external environment,[172] related to the 3-Category Violence Model. To the extent that a person achieves greater control over their own financial well-being, whether by saving more or earning more, the benefit is not only to the person having greater control over their external circumstances but also greater control over the ability to not impulsively spend money and have greater control over their future financial self. Nevertheless, rigorous research is still needed to figure out whether financial literacy interventions that are targeted for specific populations relate to reduced criminal or violent behavior. In other words, although research shows that financial interventions can lead to a person having more money— and research shows that having less money predicts violence—there is a need to connect the dots and determine whether financial interventions that do increase savings, in fact, translate to less violence.

Enhancing Employment and Work Outcomes

Related to financial well-being is one's work environment. It is difficult to overstate the economic and emotional impact of work environments on people's lives. Work is where people spend most of their waking time. It is where people earn a living and usually how they obtain health insurance, retirement benefits, life insurance, disability insurance, and in some cases childcare. Work is where people find purpose, form deep relationships, find validation and support, develop their potential, and hone their life's structure and rhythm. Thus, the financial and emotional stakes of work are extremely high and can significantly influence feelings of control over one's life and reduce external risk factors for violence.

It is not surprising, then, that aggrieved and troubled people sometimes act out their most violent impulses against their coworkers. Management and human resources departments, collaborating closely with employee assistance programs, could intervene in situations involving unfairness, harassment, intimidation, declining work performance, substance abuse, overwhelming personal stress, or threats against others.[173] Supporting and stabilizing people at work provides a foundation of empowerment and confidence, increasing the odds that they will discuss and manage violent thoughts and feelings before they become violent actions.

Can helping people with employment outcomes reduce violence? Large-scale policies to introduce employment programs on a societal scale have had mixed results in reducing violence, in part because it is difficult to know whether results are due to the employment programs or other factors.[165] What is needed are tightly controlled experiments to enable causal interpretation of the effects of jobs on violence.

In a study published in the journal *Science*, researchers conducted a randomized controlled trial of a summer jobs program for 1634 disadvantaged high school students attending high-violence schools.[174] Half of these students were assigned to an eight-week part-time summer job at a local community organization along with a job mentor. This was the experimental group. There was a second level of randomization within the experimental group, and half of the students received a summer job *and* social-emotional learning training to manage thoughts, emotions, and behaviors that could potentially interfere with their employment. The students assigned to the control group were not enrolled in the summer job program or social-emotional learning training. So, in total, there were three study conditions: (1) summer job; (2) summer job plus social-emotional learning training; and (3) neither summer job nor social-emotional learning training.

The researchers followed students for 16 months to see whether violent crime arrests were different based on which of these three study conditions they were assigned to. What did they find? The study found that students in groups 1 and 2 had significantly fewer violent crime arrests in the next 16 months compared to students in group 3. Specifically, students with summer jobs were 43% less likely to be violent in the next 16 months compared to students who had not received a summer job. Relevant to the 3-Category Violence Model, students in the experimental group who did *not* receive the extra social-emotional learning training (group 1) showed lower rates of violent crime compared to the control group (group 3). Put simply, *students attending high-violence schools were less likely to be violent if they had a summer job.* Not only did having a job provide additional income to reduce financial strain; it also provided students with a different social environment in which they could accomplish occupational goals and objectives.

That said, the study is also especially relevant because they found that students in high-violence schools who got summer jobs *and* received the extra social-emotional learning training did the best. From the vantage point of the 3-Category Violence Model, disadvantaged youth who had an intervention addressing both external sense of control (job) and internal sense of control (social-emotional learning) demonstrated the greatest reductions in violence risk and violent crime. As the authors note, their intervention had the most substantial effect on violent crime as compared to other kinds of crimes, noting that the fact that intervention "only reduces violent crime is perhaps most consistent with a role for improvements in self-control, social information processing, and decision-making, which . . . are more central to violent behavior than to other types of crime."[174(p1222)] In this way, the study shows that interventions addressing multiple domains of violence risk factors will be most effective. Again, this is consistent with our argument that addressing only a single violence risk factor will only go so far.

From the standpoint of the students who had summer jobs, not only did they receive more income and find themselves in different social environments in which they were rewarded for being productive, but they also achieved greater self-efficacy and self-worth for contributing to occupational goals and objectives. As with financial strain, more research is needed to determine whether job interventions, in fact, translate to less violence.

Building Positive Social Support and Curbing Family Violence

So far, we have reviewed interventions and policies that have promised to reduce external risk factors within the neighborhood environment, financial environment, and work environment. What, then, of the family environment? As we have seen, history of physical abuse or witnessing parental discord was shown to be related to violence risk. This translates to environments in which an individual perceives less emotional support from family and friends, itself related to violence.[83]

But it must be acknowledged that changing this situation has challenges. Stable support networks and their array of deep mutual rewards require multiple voluntary participants and take time to develop. The foundational steps are being a good family member, coworker, neighbor, and friend—and reaching out to others who are isolated. From there, larger affiliations like religious, charitable, and civic organizations can provide cohesion and support. And political organization and action, as always, will be vital in crafting laws and policies that will help keep everyone safer.

Do interventions that target social support improve outcomes for children, adults, and families? The answer is yes. Interventions have been shown to be effective, including family therapy, group therapy, parenting programs, and other support groups to improve one's social support network, including family and friends. A comprehensive literature review covering the years 2000 to 2014 found that family therapy and family interventions like parent training and behavioral programs were both affordable and effective in reducing multiple clinical problems of childhood and adolescence.[175] A companion review found these types of interventions also led to improved outcomes for adults, too.[176]

While family and parenting interventions can improve social functioning outcomes, have studies shown these interventions to reduce violence? One area to consider is related to intimate partner violence (IPV), which is associated not only with relationship instability but bad parenting.[177] Given that family discord may involve verbal or physical aggression, what has the science found regarding the ability to reduce perpetuation of intimate partner violence?

There have been multiple meta-analyses on this topic.[178-182] The answer is mixed. On the one hand, some meta-analyses show no effects. Examining substance abuse among males, a review found that "little evidence exists for effective interventions for male IPV perpetrators who use substances."[181(p1262)] On the other hand, another review found "various intervention programs are effective in reducing violence for male perpetrators of intimate partner violence comparing post to pre intervention . . . subgroup analysis revealed that incorporating substance abuse and trauma augmented treatments."[178(p220)] Similarly, couples therapy was found to be effective in reducing IPV.[179]

Why mixed findings? One clue comes from a review that specifically focused on interventions tailored to the specific risks, needs, and responsivity of the participants (as opposed to one size fits all) and also discerned whether IPV was reduced in the short term versus the long term.[182] This review found that IPV in the experimental group was 48% less in the first year after the intervention than the control group, and 40% less in the two years after the intervention than in the control group. However, after two years, this difference disappeared. Thus, distinct types of IPV treatment may be effective for varying lengths of time.

Another clue comes from a review that specifically examined another dimension of IPV interventions: treatment dropout.[180] Many perpetrators of IPV do not actually complete treatment, which in the clinical research could skew results that end up only examining pre- versus posttreatment benefits among participants who complete treatment. The authors found that "IPV offenders receiving interventions with motivational strategies were 1.73 times less likely to drop out compared to those in interventions without such strategies. For physical and psychological IPV and official recidivism (e.g., rearrests, police record), evidence favored interventions with motivational strategies, although not significantly."[180(p175)] In other words, studies may have mixed findings if they do not address this variable of treatment dropout.

Outside of IPV, do other interventions addressing social support help reduce violence? A 2017 meta-analysis examined whether parenting programs were effective in reducing recidivism of child physical abuse.[145] This review only selected randomized controlled trials and only families referred from Child Protective Services who had documented child physical abuse, meaning that studies were all high quality and ensured the participants were representative. They found child physical abuse recidivism was 11% lower for families who received behavioral parenting training based on social-learning theory. They concluded, "The results of this review suggest that behavioral parenting programs are modestly but significantly effective strategies for reducing hard markers of recidivism in physically abusive families."[145(p362)]

Parent interventions have the potential to reduce child physical abuse but can also help reduce children's criminal behavior. A longitudinal study examined the effects of an established preventive intervention, The Child-Parent Center (CPC), on outcomes in over 1500 young adult participants nearly 20 years after the study began.[183] Close to 1000 participants received the CPC intervention, which delivered educational and family-support services until third grade, emphasized language arts and math skills, included a parent-resource teacher coordinating family support as well as a paraprofessional school-community representative providing outreach to families, ensured low child-to-staff ratios, offered parenting education, and provided health services, food services, speech therapy, and nurse referrals. A comparison group of 550 participants was studied on age, neighborhood, and family poverty. The findings nearly 20 years after study enrollment provided solid evidence of early interventions: the CPC preschool participants were more likely to go to college and be employed full time and were less likely to have felony arrests, convictions, incarceration, and arrests for violent offenses.

Reviewing this and other "sociobehavioral" interventions, epidemiologist Charles Branas concludes: "A fundamental aspect and benefit of many of these interventions is that, with thoughtful implementation, they may also address the most basic upstream causes of gun violence, such as structural racism, poverty, housing inequity, unemployment, and educational inequality."[184(p244)] This observation comports with the 3-Category Violence Model in that it seeks to prioritize addressing social determinants and environment-level risk factors that increase risk of violence. Policymakers are in the position to research and implement many of these strategies on an environment-level scale, which the review of risk factors shows is a critical component to address for effectively preventing violence.

8

Preventing Violence: Strategies for Reducing Individual-Level Risk Factors

Improving Anger Management and Emotion Regulation

A first step in reducing internal risk factors would be to address anger management, as anger has been shown to be a strong predictor of violence in the NESARC and MacArthur Violence Risk Assessment Study and in the meta-analysis of risk factors for intimate partner violence.[23,30,134] For a long time, scientific literature reviews and meta-analyses[185,186] have found medium-to-large effect sizes across different modalities of counseling and therapy for reducing anger problems, particularly cognitive behavioral therapy (CBT) for anger.

A manual for a 12-session CBT program for Anger Management is published by the Substance Abuse and Mental Health Services Administration (SAMHSA),[187] which has made PDFs available, updated in 2019, for clinicians and with workbooks available for patients. This manualized anger management treatment focuses on teaching relaxation skills, cognitive restructuring, and assertive communication skills.

What does this treatment look like? The American Psychological Association provides an excellent synopsis of what to expect from anger management treatment: "If you see a psychologist for help with anger problems, you can plan on examining the triggers that set you off. You'll explore how your experiences of anger were helpful or harmful, both in the short-term and in the long-term. You'll probably examine the thoughts that precede your anger and explore whether they're accurate assessments of reality. Psychologists may also help you to learn to resolve conflicts in a more constructive way and rebuild relationships that have been damaged by your anger."[188]

Despite the promise of anger management treatment generally, and CBT specifically, for addressing violence risk, it is critical to note that, given all the other risk factors described in this book, treating anger alone may not be enough to prevent violence. Indeed, a 2018 review of meta-analyses concluded: "Anger treatments have consistently demonstrated at least moderate effectiveness among both non-clinical and psychiatric populations, whereas aggression treatment results have been less consistent."[189(p65)] This suggests that mixed findings regarding anger treatment being effective as the sole means to reduce aggression unless other violence risk factors (such as those discussed throughout this book) are also addressed.

Nevertheless, with respect to reducing violence and related criminal behavior, a meta-analysis[190] showed that *CBT-based anger management in adults achieved a risk reduction of 23% for general criminal recidivism and 28% for violent criminal recidivism.* Correspondingly, they found that CBT treatment completion resulted in a 42% risk reduction in general criminal recidivism and a 56% risk reduction in violent criminal recidivism. In children, a comprehensive, meta-analytic synthesis of the literature using a total of 60 studies from 1979 to 2010 showed an overall effect size of −0.27, which translates to a small-to-medium effect of anger management intervention reducing anger, aggression, and loss of self-control.[191] Regardless, measuring violence as an outcome is the critical next step needed in clinical research on anger management, and randomized controlled trial designs are also needed to figure out whether or to what extent interventions lead to a reduction in anger and violence.

Anger is one part of a broader concept of emotional dysregulation, whereas stress comprises another part. In the past two decades, effective stress management has been the goal of mindfulness-based interventions. Mindfulness-based interventions involve the practice of being aware of oneself and one's situation in the present moment through meditation: seated or in slow movement. Mindfulness exercises might include deep breathing or focusing on, for example, the body or the breath.

Mindfulness can be used by anyone and is largely based on ancient Buddhist meditation practice. There are hundreds of mobile apps enabling users to conduct mindfulness exercises anywhere at any time. These exercises can be practiced alone or with others, for as little as a few minutes each day. Research confirms that mindfulness offers spiritual, emotional, cognitive, and physical benefits. In a comprehensive meta-analysis on mindfulness-based therapies, the authors reviewed over 200 studies testing whether mindfulness improved outcomes for those who completed training.[192] The authors found that mindfulness-based therapies had moderate effect sizes for reducing anxiety symptoms and depressive symptoms. Of note, these therapeutic benefits were found to continue well after treatment was completed.

Do these findings also encompass aggression and violent behavior? In a systematic review of the effect of mindfulness on violence and aggression in adults, authors reviewed 22 studies including 14 randomized trials.[193] They found that although more good quality-controlled studies are needed to confirm results, mindfulness-based interventions would be postulated to be effective in reducing aggression and violence through improved ability to regulate emotions.

For example, in one study examining the effect of mindfulness on reducing aggression,[194] participants were randomized to one of two groups. In the experimental group, participants received training programs including breathing exercises, monitoring thoughts or feelings in one's mind, noticing if one's mind is wandering, and taking on a nonjudgmental attitude toward one's self and others. In the control group, participants were asked to solve logic problems including geometric puzzles, word problems, and analogies. Both types of sessions took the same amount of time and had the same number of sessions. The study found that in an experimental measure of aggression where the participant is provoked, those in the mindfulness group were significantly less likely to engage in aggressive behavior compared to those in the control group. One limitation is that this regards aggressive behavior enacted in the context of a research laboratory as opposed to real life. As noted in the comprehensive literature review,[193] more work is needed to see if mindfulness leads to significant reductions in violent behavior as measured not only in a laboratory but also in real-world settings.

A systematic review of mindfulness-based interventions on aggression in children and adolescents, involving a meta-analysis of existing studies,[195] found 18 studies meeting inclusion criteria; unfortunately, only three were randomized controlled trials. The meta-analysis results showed an overall moderate effect size for mindfulness-based interventions reducing aggressiveness in children and adolescents. However, the authors note limitations in the existing literature including the need to study distinct types of aggression including physical aggression and to include more rigorous methodologies including randomized controlled trials.

Addressing this very limitation, one study[196] randomly assigned elementary school students to a mindfulness-based educational intervention that included a focus on attention and self-control or to a waitlist control group (meaning the children eventually received the intervention but at first did not). This way, the researchers were able to compare the students who received the intervention to those on the waitlist. In this case, the researchers found a positive effect of mindfulness-based interventions on reducing children's actual aggressive behavior in school and on improving their ability to have cognitive self-control, as observed in class.

The current science on the effects of mindfulness in children, adolescents, and adults for reducing aggression is promising. The upside of mindfulness training is that it is accessible, cost effective, able to be incorporated into mobile technology, and has a rapidly growing evidence base. It can also be combined with many other kinds of interventions quite readily. Currently, there is still the need for more randomized controlled trials that show effects on actual physical aggressive behavior to be conducted in the future.

Treating Substance Abuse and Mental Illness

In 1982, an article was published in *JAMA* (*Journal of the American Medical Association*) entitled "Is Treatment for Substance Abuse Effective?" The authors answered this question affirmatively but with qualifications.[197] The researchers followed over 700 patients who completed different substance abuse treatment programs: including a 60-day therapeutic community based on the principles of Alcoholics Anonymous (AA); a 45-day program consisting of AA, individual psychotherapy, and education; and drug abuse rehabilitation consisting of vocational counseling, group psychological therapy, and methadone maintenance combining pharmacological and individual psychotherapy. The authors found, overall, that participants after treatment had reduced alcohol and drug use and criminal behavior as well as improved employment and psychological function. While promising, the authors acknowledge that "we recognized that despite the significant improvements shown in the alcoholic and drug addict samples, there was no clear evidence that the changes were a result of the treatment process. We needed a comparison group as a control for nontreatment factors."[197(p1427)]

Since then, hundreds of scientific studies have incorporated comparison groups and conducted randomized controlled trials of substance abuse treatment, and many approaches have been proven to be effective at reducing substance use. For alcohol misuse, the National Institute on Alcohol Abuse and Alcoholism (NIAAA) states: "The good news is that no matter how severe the problem may seem, most people with AUD [alcohol use disorder] can benefit from some form of treatment. Research shows that about one-third of people who are treated for alcohol problems have no further symptoms 1 year later. Many others substantially reduce their drinking and report fewer alcohol-related problems."[198] According to the NIAAA, the effective options for addressing alcohol misuse are Behavioral Treatments (Cognitive–Behavioral Therapy, Motivational Enhancement Therapy, Marital and Family Counseling, and Brief Interventions), Medications (Naltrexone, Acamprosate, Disulfiram), and Mutual-Support Groups (AA and other 12-step programs).[198]

Correspondingly, for drug misuse, the National Institute on Drug Abuse (NIDA) states, "According to research that tracks individuals in treatment over extended periods, most people who get into and remain in treatment stop using drugs, decrease their criminal activity, and improve their occupational, social, and psychological functioning. For example, methadone treatment has been shown to increase participation in behavioral therapy and decrease both drug use and criminal behavior."[199] The effective treatment options for treating drug misuse include group therapy (contingency management that promotes a non-drug-using lifestyle), behavioral treatments (cognitive-behavioral therapy), and treatment medications (methadone, buprenorphine, and naltrexone). NIDA adds that "because they work on different aspects of addiction, combinations of behavioral therapies and medications (when available) generally appear to be more effective than either approach used alone."[199]

That a combination of therapy and medication is more effective applies to the treatment of mental illness, as well. For example, describing treatment for schizophrenia, NIMH indicates that "antipsychotic medications can help make psychotic symptoms less intense and less frequent" and "people who participate in regular psychosocial treatment are less likely to have symptoms reoccur or to be hospitalized. Examples of this kind of treatment include cognitive behavioral therapy, behavioral skills training, supported employment, and cognitive remediation interventions."[200] The NIMH indicates that medications and psychosocial treatments are often used together and are effective for schizophrenia, as well as for bipolar disorder and major depressive disorder. Overall, given the current state of science, substance abuse and mental illness are optimally treated with medication and psychosocial therapy delivered in tandem.

Nevertheless, it is unclear whether any of this translates to preventing violent behavior. NIDA, NIAAA, and NIMH do not explicitly say that treatment leads to reduced violence, though NIDA is closest by writing that treatment leads to reduced criminal behavior. What is known about whether treatment of substance abuse and mental illness leads to reduced violence?

For alcohol, one study examined intimate partner violence after the delivery of alcoholism treatment for 301 male outpatients who abused alcohol. The study found that in the year before treatment, 56% of the outpatients had been violent toward their female partner while in the year after treatment, violence decreased to 25%.[201] Although promising, this study involved a single armed clinical trial, meaning there was no control group.

With respect to randomized trials, in a study of adolescents aged 14 to 18 years who presented to an emergency department and reported alcohol use and aggression in the past year,[202] participants were randomized either to an experimental group (receiving a brief 35-minute intervention by computer or a therapist) or to a control group (receiving a brochure). The brief intervention was delivered in the emergency department, and involved role plays, motivational interviewing, skills training, review of personal goals, and community services referrals. *The authors found that adolescents who received the brief intervention were 34% less likely to perpetrate aggression toward peers in the following three months than previously*, which represented a much larger reduction in violence compared to adolescents who did not receive the brief intervention. That said, limitations included self-report of aggression and limited benefit on reducing violence outcomes at six months.

Further, the literature has not consistently found effects of alcohol treatment on reduced violence. A clinical trial of partner-violent men with alcohol problems randomized participants either to brief alcohol intervention involving motivation enhancement therapy (experimental) or to receive alcohol education (control).[203] The researchers found no differences between groups with alcohol use or intimate partner violence at the end of the study. This was consistent with results of a recent meta-analysis showing no significant effects of motivational strategies for intimate partner violent offenders on reducing physical aggression.[180]

In contrast to alcohol treatment, outside of a few small studies,[204] research on effects of drug treatment on violence is needed in the literature. Similarly, studies examining effects of treatment for mental illness on violence are limited as well. We are unaware of randomized controlled trials examining the effects of mental health treatment for bipolar disorder on reduced violence. Although not a randomized trial, longitudinal data in patients with schizophrenia and bipolar disorder showed that "compared with periods when participants were not on medication, violent crime fell by 45% in patients receiving antipsychotics . . . and by 24% in patients prescribed mood stabilisers."[205(p1206)] The authors do note that randomized controlled trials of pharmacological intervention to reduce violence have obstacles, including difficulty recruiting individuals who have higher aggressiveness or hostility and ethical challenges of immediate safety needs among participants who may be at acute high risk of violence.

With respect to schizophrenia, in a double-blinded randomized controlled trial, 1445 individuals with schizophrenia were randomly assigned to one of five antipsychotic medications. The study found that "no difference by medication group was found, except that perphenazine showed greater violence reduction than quetiapine in the retained sample. Medication adherence reduced violence but not in patients with a history of childhood antisocial conduct."[92] A recent review reports on two randomized controlled trials that clozapine decreases aggressiveness in patients with schizophrenia compared to the other treatments.[206] Beyond these few studies, a literature review finds no other randomized controlled trials for treatments to reduce violence in schizophrenia.

Also, we did not find randomized controlled trials examining the effects of mental health treatment for major depression on reduced violence.

One potential reason for mixed findings in the limited research that has been done could stem from the fact that many studies enroll individuals with substance abuse or mental illness, but not both. As shown in Chapter 4, it is *co-occurring* mental illness and substance abuse that is consistently related to violence across multiple studies. So, what is known about treatment for co-occurring mental illness and substance use disorders? A review of 45 studies found positive effects of interventions (e.g., group counseling, residential treatment, case management, and legal intervention) in the lives of people with co-occurring mental illness and substance use disorder.[207] There is also evidence that computer-based interventions (CBT, psychoeducation, social feedback, and support) are effective adjuncts to traditional clinical treatment for co-occurring mental illness and substance use disorder.[208]

We are aware of limited research that have examined the effect of treatment for co-occurring mental illness and substance use disorder on reduced violence. In one study, individuals who have co-occurring mental illness and substance use disorder and who engage in intimate partner violence are less likely to complete substance abuse treatment.[209] This finding reveals that this subgroup of individuals is less likely to adhere to treatment and may be more difficult to engage.

This lack of treatment engagement is problematic given a systemic challenge that needs to be addressed at a policy level: treatment for both mental illness and substance abuse rarely occur concurrently. Typically, mental health and substance abuse clinics are separate, often siloed from one another even within the same facility. Data from 2019 reveal that only a fraction (12.7%) of people with co-occurring disorders receive treatment for both.[210] As a result, the subgroup of individuals most at risk of violence is also the subgroup getting suboptimal treatment, most typically addressing only half the problem. This is confirmed by a review of treatments, showing that despite the high co-prevalence of substance abuse and mental illness, "single disorder guidelines did not adequately recommend the importance of diagnosis or treatment of concurrent disorders despite their high co-prevalence."[211]

As a result, there is a desperate need for more treatment of co-occurring mental illness and substance misuse, especially given that people with mental illness experience substance use disorders at triple the rate of people without mental illness.[111] This is especially troubling as recent data from SAMHSA indicate that co-occurring substance abuse and mental illness have been increasing in the United States.[212]

Addressing Trauma, Abuse, and Bullying

This category addresses internal and external factors because it is related to one feeling unsafe in a social environment. Eighty percent of perpetrators of targeted school violence had been bullied by classmates, and physical abuse was a predictor of violence in multiple studies. It is important to recognize that just because a person is a victim of abuse does not mean they will be violent; rather, a history of witnessing violence or being abused and bullied elevates the risk of being violent. The literature review shows that it is critical to address any history of trauma and being abused, including being bullied, which as we have seen relates to higher risk of violence.

For this reason, policies at schools, workplaces, and in social service agencies that target addressing trauma, before it festers, should be a core component of violence prevention strategies. Fortunately, research has shown that multiple interventions are effective in improving outcomes for people who have been traumatized or who meet criteria for posttraumatic stress disorder (PTSD).[213] Although people in the mental health field are aware of these, it is important to convey to the general public that trauma treatment can be effective. The American Psychological Association strongly recommends several psychotherapies:

- Cognitive behavioral therapy, which focuses on the relationships among thoughts, feelings and behaviors; targets current problems and symptoms; and focuses on changing patterns of behaviors, thoughts and feelings that lead to difficulties in functioning. Cognitive behavioral therapy notes how changes in any one domain can improve functioning in the other domains. For example, altering a person's unhelpful thinking can lead to healthier behaviors and improved emotion regulation. It is typically delivered over 12–16 sessions in either individual or group format.[214]

- Cognitive processing therapy, which is a specific type of cognitive behavioral therapy that helps patients learn how to modify and challenge unhelpful beliefs related to the trauma. CPT is generally delivered over 12 sessions and helps patients learn how to challenge and modify unhelpful beliefs related to the trauma. In so doing, the patient creates a new understanding and conceptualization of the traumatic event so that it reduces its ongoing negative effects on current life.[214]

- Prolonged exposure, which is a specific type of cognitive behavioral therapy that teaches individuals to gradually approach trauma-related memories, feelings, and situations. By facing what has been avoided, a person presumably learns that the trauma-related memories and cues are not dangerous and do not need to be avoided. Typically provided over a period of about three months with weekly individual sessions. Sixty- to 120-minute sessions are usually needed in order for the individual to engage in exposure and sufficiently process the experience.[214]

There has been a tremendous amount of research examining these psychological treatments for PTSD. In adults who have experienced trauma, meta-analyses, and comprehensive literature reviews have found that individual trauma-focused cognitive behavioral therapy, cognitive processing therapy, and exposure therapy are effective in the treatment of PTSD.[215,216] CBT was found to be effective at reducing acute stress disorder shortly after exposure to trauma, meaning that early intervention has benefits.[217] Correspondingly, a recent article reviewing the evidence base for psychosocial treatments for traumatized children and adolescents reviewed studies and evaluated for methodological rigor; the study found there were benefits from CBT and psychosocial treatment after the following types of traumas: man-made and natural disasters, bullying and cyberbullying, and childhood abuse.[218]

In this regard, attention to bullying, a pattern of harassment and intimidation instead of a single conflict, is crucial to mitigate future violence. As suggested by the USSS report on Targeted School Violence, victims of bullying often become isolated, emotionally hurt, angry, and filled with violent fantasies of revenge. Teachers, counselors, and administrators should intervene early when they detect bullying, working with both the victim and the perpetrator to define limits and consequences, provide support, enhance understanding and coping skills, and improve relationships.

Little of the research on interventions to treat trauma symptoms has examined its effects on reducing violent behavior. That said, it is important to recognize that the link between trauma, PTSD, and perpetration of violence is complex. One study examined nationally representative longitudinal data of the NESARC to figure out whether a diagnosis of PTSD before the first wave of data collection predicted violent behavior in the next three years measured at the second wave of data collection.[114] The authors found that PTSD was associated with elevated violent behavior if the participant became angry after the trauma or used alcohol to self-medicate anxiety due to the trauma. Put differently, PTSD diagnosis alone, absent anger or self-medication, did not significantly predict violence. As a result, future research on the use of trauma treatment to reduce violent behavior should address components of the interventions on anger management and alcohol treatment discussed earlier in this chapter. Policies that allocate funds to schools, mental health agencies, and social service systems to expand training clinicians to implement these clinical practices (shown to be effective) are warranted to help diminish the societal impact of adverse events.

9

Preventing Violence: Strategies for Reducing Viability and Acceptability of Violence

Modifying Criminal Thinking and Preventing Antisocial Behavior

Although a meta-analysis from several decades ago suggested that psychopathic traits and antisocial behavior could be treated,[219] the review did not report that randomized controlled trial study designs had been used in research and indicated that well-controlled experimental designs were necessary. Indeed, a 2020 Cochrane Systematic Review of psychological treatment for antisocial personality disorder (AsPD) concluded: "There is very limited evidence available on psychological interventions for adults with AsPD . . . No intervention reported compelling evidence of change in antisocial behaviour. Overall, the certainty of the evidence was low or very low, meaning that we have little confidence in the effect estimates reported."[220(p1)]

That said, there are promising avenues for interventions addressing cognitive components of antisocial personality disorder: criminal thinking patterns and lack of empathy. Criminal thinking patterns involve the belief that it is justifiable to break the law for one's own purposes or that it is justifiable to hurt someone physically who has angered them. Lack of empathy is a key component of acts of violence because it involves lack of concern about inflicting harm on another person—not considering how it would feel for that person to experience severe physical pain.

There have been several clinical trials that have been successful at reducing criminal thinking, although they do have study limitations. In one such study, over 200 male prisoners completed a ten-week intervention called "lifestyle issues" in which prisoners were taught about developmental and behavioral components of criminal lifestyles, criminal thinking patterns that supported this lifestyle, and multiple ways to challenge criminal thinking styles.[221] The intervention was delivered in group format. The authors found that prisoners who showed lower scores on a measure of criminal thinking were significantly less likely to engage in institutional misconduct—which presumably included violent infractions—in the next year compared to prisoners who did not show this change from the intervention.

A similar research design was used when researchers tested the effectiveness of an intervention targeting criminal thinking called "Taking a Chance on Change" in 273 prison inmates.[222] This intervention involved multiple components, including goal setting; identifying and changing mistaken beliefs; effective problem solving; communication of emotion, anger, and stress management; and relapse prevention. These components consisted of handouts and worksheets that inmates completed over the course of nine to 12 months. Parallel to the earlier study, researchers in this study showed that inmates who completed this intervention had reductions in their criminal thinking and in institutional misconduct.

Replication of scientific findings across two independent studies with the same target of modifying criminal thinking patterns gives greater confidence in the results. But while these findings show some promise for this approach, it cannot be confidently concluded that the interventions led to the change in criminal thinking and reduced institutional misconduct because neither study used randomized controlled trials. As a result, one cannot definitively attribute benefits to the intervention itself. These studies also could not control for selection bias, meaning it is possible only certain categories of inmates completed the intervention.

In this regard, a different group of researchers did conduct a randomized controlled trial to determine if an intervention could promote changes in empathy among perpetrators of intimate partner violence.[223] In this study, perpetrators of intimate partner violence were randomized into two groups. In the control group, participants received a standard batterer intervention program while in the experimental group, participants received the same standard batterer intervention program plus facilitation of an individualized motivational plan to increase treatment adherence, address motivation for change, and identify personal goals for change. Both consisted of 30 weekly two-hour group sessions. Analysis revealed that the intimate partner violence perpetrators who received the experimental intervention performed better on measures of empathy, specifically the facet of empathy concerned with being able to appreciate another person's perspective. Participants in the experimental group were more accurate identifying emotions of others by facial signals and scored higher on a measure of empathic perspective-taking than participants in the control group.

While this study enrolled individuals at risk of violence, there have been other perspective-taking interventions that aim to increase empathy,[224] encouraging individuals to better understand the feelings of others, such as patients with life-threatening illnesses or individuals experiencing homelessness. Recently, studies have begun to capitalize on virtual reality technology to effectively improve empathy among participants, finding that virtual reality technology can help induce prosocial behavior, reverse racial bias, and decrease prejudice.

In one such study conducted at Stanford University, 180 participants were provided with handheld controllers to interact with a virtual environment.[225] When they interacted with objects, participants were provided feedback by vibrations through their hand controllers. The purpose of this feedback was to increase participants' immersion in the virtual environment.

Participants were randomized to one of three different virtual reality experiences. In the control group, participants walked around a virtual environment depicting the lab room. In the other two study conditions, participants "virtually" took the perspective of a student who attended the same university. Participants had an equal chance of embodying the avatars of either "Steve" or "James," who were two fictional characters with similar but not entirely identical backgrounds.

After completing the virtual reality intervention, participants answered a questionnaire and were told their answers were going to be "paired" to another student's answers. The participants were randomly assigned to be paired with Steve or James, regardless of group assignment. As a result, the experimenters were able to divide the sample into three conditions: (1) *"indirect empathy"* for participants who embodied a different avatar than who they were paired with for the questionnaire, (2) *"direct empathy"* for participants who embodied the same avatar with whom they were paired with for the questionnaire, and (3) *"control"* for participants who embodied no avatar but were still paired with Steve or James.

The hypothesis was that perspective-taking experiences through virtual reality would increase prosocial behavior. The researchers made two discoveries: First, they found that participants' inclination to consider the perspective of others was highest in the direct empathy group. Second, effects on perspective-taking were even higher the more participants were immersed in the virtual reality environment.

Although this study involved college students, the results provide strong evidence with a randomized controlled trial that virtual reality can be used effectively to improve perspective-taking, a key facet of empathy. Together, while studies addressing criminal thinking and lacking empathy through interventions are needed that enroll individuals with antisocial personality disorder and criminal thinking and to see if these changes lead to less engagement in violent behavior.

The above interventions primarily change criminal *thinking* and perspective-taking, whereas other approaches exist that primarily aim to curb *behavior* that is disruptive, criminal, or violent.

First, an intervention called the "Good Behavior Game" (GBG) has shown promise in reducing aggression in adolescents.[226] Called a "behavioral vaccine,"[227] GBG is based on behavioral principles of reinforcement. It provides contingencies after the occurrence of prosocial or antisocial behaviors. A teacher divides a class into two teams. Over the course of a day, the teacher gives points to the team if one of its members engages in disruptive or aggressive behavior. The team with the fewest number of points at the end of that day gets rewarded. But also if the two teams fall below a preset level of points at the end of the day, then all players from both teams share in the reward. This approach has shown moderate to strong effects of GBG on reducing problem behaviors, including aggression.[228] Positive effects of GBG were confirmed by meta-analyses though it was noted that effect sizes differed by outcome and sex (e.g., girls did better than boys on reduction in teacher-rated conduct problems).[226] Future work on the GBG is needed to focus even more on components related to specific outcomes such as aggression and violence. For now, it is important to recognize that the effects of GBG correspond to the 3-Category Violence Model in that the contingencies and rewards of the intervention simultaneously make it less acceptable to be aggressive and more acceptable to be prosocial.

Second, although there is mixed evidence that treatment is effective for reducing risk of sexual assault and sex offenses, a comprehensive review does indicate that some treatment is effective for some types of offenders in some settings.[229] A Campbell Systematic Review found: "On average, there is a significant reduction in recidivism rates in the treated groups. The odds to sexually reoffend were 1.41 lower for treated compared to control groups. This equals a sexual recidivism rate of 10.1 percent for treated offenders compared to 13.7 percent without treatment. The mean rates for general recidivism were higher but showed a similar reduction of roughly a quarter due to treatment."[230(p5)] Nevertheless, the authors found that the setting of treatment delivery mattered: in the community and forensic setting, treatment was found to be effective whereas sex offender treatment was not found to be effective when delivered in prison settings. Additionally, they note "cognitive-behavioral foundation of treatment has relatively good potential, but other features, like the risk of the treated offenders or including individualized treatment, significantly affect treatment success."[229] Finally, they cautioned that methodology between studies was too varied to draw conclusions about the effectiveness of sex offender treatment, calling for more rigorous research using randomized controlled trial study designs.

Third, with respect to curbing criminal and violent behavior, family interventions that address environment- and individual-level factors in juvenile offenders have been shown to reduce antisocial and violent behavior. One example is Multisystemic Therapy (MST), which involves treatment that blends environment-level (e.g., delivering services in the juvenile offenders' home, school, and neighborhood) and individual-level (e.g., delivering evidence-based cognitive behavioral therapy or family therapy) factors. A randomized trial enrolling juvenile offenders showed that MST led to not only reduced criminal behavior among juvenile offenders but also to benefits among their siblings, who were found to have been significantly less likely to have engaged in criminal behavior during the course of the 25 years after the intervention was implemented.[229] The authors of this research acknowledge other evidence-based treatments (e.g., multidimensional foster care and functional family therapy) that similarly benefit by addressing environment and individual level factors. They conclude that "treatments that fail to target the multiple causes and correlates of antisocial behavior in a youth's social ecology" [229(p.498)] are unlikely to yield optimal benefit. This research is consistent with the organization of risk factors in the 3-Category Violence Model.

Fourth, the past two decades have shown the promise of multidisciplinary threat assessment teams for preventing targeted violence.[231] Threat assessment teams are often located in schools or in the workplace.[232,233] Rather than target factors specifically using a predictive risk assessment approach, these teams investigate reported threats and develop responses gauged to the seriousness of the threat and potential perpetrator's needs (as well as risk factors). For example, threat assessment teams analyze the severity and likelihood of threatening communications and behaviors in order to formulate a violence prevention strategy individualized for the potential perpetrator.[234] There is evidence these teams can avert violence in schools[233] and workplaces.[173] Randomized trials comparing different models of threat assessment teams and identifying their core components most strongly related to reduced violence would be an important next step in the scientific literature to determine the effectiveness of threat assessment teams in preventing violence. School and workplace policies can improve safety by developing threat assessment teams while policymakers and law enforcement agencies can provide education, research support, and work collaboratively with these teams to improve effectiveness.

Promoting Gun Safety and Safe Storage of Firearms

Between 2009 and 2017, epidemiological research reports there was a recorded average of over 110,000 emergency room visits for firearm injuries per year (85,700 nonfatalities plus 34,500 deaths) in the United States.[235] As shown in the science reviewed in previous chapters, access to weapons and interest in weapons ranked among top risk factors for violence. Direct access to a gun had a very large effect size on homicide for intimate partner violence among male perpetrators, ranked number 1 out of 13 risk factors and history of using weapons was ranked number 3 out of 34 risk factors for targeted school violence. Over three-quarters of perpetrators of targeted school violence acquired their firearms from the homes of relatives or friends. Over half of perpetrators who attacked government officials or buildings had previously used firearms.

A critical aspect of extreme violence and mass shootings is availability of firearms and their proliferation. The most lethal thing most people can wield are guns, especially high-powered, semi-automatic ones. What do empirical studies show about policies to reduce gun violence and increase gun safety? In a time series analysis reviewing the link between the restrictiveness of state gun laws in the United States and mass shootings using the Federal Bureau of Investigation's uniform crime reporting system, spanning from 1998 to 2015.[236] The researchers found that States that had more permissive gun laws also had 11.5% higher rates of mass shootings in that same period. Moreover, they found a correlation between gun ownership and rate of mass shootings: a 10% increase in gun ownership in a given state was linked to a 35% increase in mass shootings in that state. The more people owned guns, enabling violence to be a viable option, the more likely violence was to be perpetrated, consistent with the 3-Category Violence Model.

These findings are consistent with another analysis examining whether there were changes in firearm mortality after implementation of state laws reducing or increasing access to firearms.[237] This study looked at changes in state-level policies from 1970 to 2016. The researchers found that Child Access Prevention (CAP) laws were associated with a lower death rate. Correspondingly, right to carry (RTC) and stand your ground (SYG) laws were associated with a higher death rate. Combined, the authors conclude: "The joint effects of these laws indicate that the restrictive gun policy regime (having a CAP law without an RTC or SYG law) has a 0.98 probability of being associated with a reduction in firearm-related deaths relative to the permissive policy regime. This estimated effect corresponds to an 11% reduction in firearm related deaths relative to the permissive legal regime."[237(p117)] Similar results were found with a comprehensive review of the science conducted by the RAND Corporation in which states that had stand-your-ground laws—associated with more permissive gun laws and policy—were related to an increase in the total number of homicides.[238] These findings also support our theory that violent behavior increases when it is a more viable option for the perpetrator.

Nevertheless, the RAND report also showed that there is inconclusive evidence regarding whether other gun safety interventions reduce violent crime. When subjected to a rigorous evidence-based review, the RAND report[238] determined the following effects on violent crime were "inconclusive": surrender of firearms by prohibited possessors, background checks, extreme risk protection orders, firearms sales reporting, licensing and permitting requirements, firearms safety training, lost or stolen firearm reporting requirements, bans on the sale of assault weapons and high capacity magazines, bans on low-quality handguns, gun-free zones, and laws allowing armed staff in K–12 schools.

Of importance, just because the findings were inconclusive does not mean that these approaches are not effective; rather, that findings were inconclusive could also mean that these approaches have not been subject to rigorous investigation to allow firm conclusions. However, the RAND report did indicate the following:

1. States with firearm prohibitions for individuals subject to domestic violence restraining orders did in fact reduce firearm-related intimate partner homicides and total number of intimate partner homicides.[238] As a result, the RAND report recommended that states without laws prohibiting gun ownership for individuals who have restraining orders associated with domestic violence should pass those laws as a strategy to reduce gun violence.

2. Background checks were associated with reduced firearm homicides, noting that this research is based on the effects of dealer background checks as opposed to private seller background checks.[238] Correspondingly, the review also found that waiting periods were linked to reduced homicides as well as firearm homicides. That background checks passed scientific rigor matches this commonsense approach to reducing violence.

3. Prohibitions related to mental illness as associated with reduced violence were found to be "inconclusive." Although research is still needed, one would hypothesize this approach would yield limited effects given the research we reviewed in Chapters 4 and 5 showing that mental illness is a weaker factor in violence than perceived.

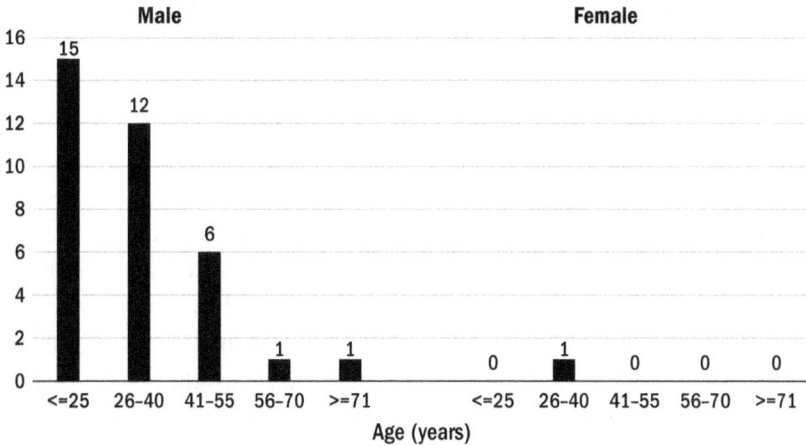

Figure 9.1: Number of Perpetrators of Mass Violence Involving Ten or More Victims in the United States since 1949, Stratified by Age and Sex. Source: Wikipedia.

The RAND report did indicate that effectiveness of minimum age requirements was inconclusive; however, there have been increasing legislative efforts to raise the age at which individuals can purchase semiautomatic weapons.[238] This is consistent with the scientific evidence presented in previous chapters demonstrating that being young is strongly associated with increased risk of violence. To illustrate, Figure 9.1 depicts the age and sex of perpetrators of the deadliest mass shootings in the United States since 1949 involving 10 or more victims.[239] Just under half (42%) were perpetrated by males 25 years old or younger. Not captured in the figure are the weapons used in these heinous crimes. Review of the data shows that virtually all of these mass shootings involved semiautomatic weapons. Keep in mind that this figure only represents the worst massacres. There are thousands more multiple-victim murders that are not included here. Yet empirical research suggests a similar pattern would emerge as being young and male remains a strong predictor of violence, as evidenced in multiple national epidemiological studies of violence in the United States.[15,23,111,112] The science of violence risk factors therefore strongly implies that raising the age at which individuals can purchase a semiautomatic rifle could prevent mass violence and save lives. In a clear example, such changes in the law would literally have averted the tragedy in Uvalde, Texas, in May 2022, when an 18-year-old who purchased two AR-15 semiautomatic rifles killed 19 elementary school children and two teachers.

Other strategies have been proposed to improve gun safety and reduce gun violence. Red flag laws enable family members, law enforcement, fellow employees, and others to petition the court in order to remove firearms temporarily from a person they believe is at risk of harming others or themselves. How the assessment of risk to others occurs is not trivial, especially given the many risk factors for violence reviewed in the earlier chapters. Empirical research has shown some potential benefits; for example, one analysis made a conservative estimate that at least 1 life was saved for every 20 firearm removals in 2 states with red-flag laws (Connecticut and Indiana).[240] Nevertheless, another study analyzing data in San Diego County, California, failed to find that firearm removal laws led to either reduced firearm violence or reduced self-harm.[241] As these laws are relatively new, and studies are limited, more state-level data analysis is needed to better inform how (or whether) this strategy prevents firearm violence.

Finally, scholars and professional medical societies have called for policies that address safer firearm storage as a standard goal[242] and promote gun cabinets and trigger locks to improve gun and firearm safety.[243] Research supports these recommendations, showing that safe-storage households are at lower risk for death, self-inflicted injury, and suicide.[244] Further, a thorough review of research on the effectiveness of safe-storage interventions suggests that specific strategies are effective; for example, authors of the review found that the distribution of free safe-firearm devices (e.g., trigger locks) was effective in improving safe storage, whereas providing economic incentives to acquire those devices was not.[245] The authors concluded that "although additional studies are needed, the totality of evidence suggests that counseling augmented by device provision can effectively encourage individuals to store their firearms safely."[245(p111)] In other words, a key approach to reducing risk of violence in society at large is to have weapons stored safely.

Recall that nearly three-quarters (74%) of perpetrators of targeted school violence in the USSS report[141] reviewed in Chapter 5 had acquired their weapons from family and friends. A national survey revealed that a little less than half of gun owners (46%) reported storing all of their guns safely.[246] Increasing the rate of safe storage, by definition, reduces access to a deadly weapon, and per the 3-Category Violence Model, reduces overall violence risk. The same study found that owning handguns and having a child in the home were significantly associated with safe gun storage. Further, gun owners indicated that gun storage decisions were significantly associated with having taken a gun safety course and having had a discussion with family members. The authors indicated: "Gun owners ranked law enforcement, hunting or outdoors groups, active-duty military, and the National Rifle Association as most effective in communicating safe storage practices."[246(p532)] As a result, the authors conclude that policies and education promoting safe gun storage, potentially in conjunction with these organizations, have the potential to save lives.

Minimizing Influence of Groups Encouraging Hate and Violence

Another critical aspect of the violence-defining factors is an individual not only having access to weapons but also believing that it is acceptable to hurt others, that a person has the "green light" to be violent. As described above, a quarter of perpetrators of targeted school violence had a specific interest in the Columbine shooting (23%) and one-fifth had a specific interest in Hitler/Nazism (20%), and as described in the case of Adam Lanza, there exists online content that at-risk individuals can access regularly if they want to. In the USSS report on risk factors associated with mass attacks in public places, it was found that nearly one-quarter (24%) of perpetrators espouse beliefs associated with hate, including anti-Semitism, white supremacy, Nazism, xenophobia, antifascism, jihadism, and anti-immigration.[144]

Online groups to promote these interests and encourage hate and violence have emerged in the past two decades. As scholars explain, "Hate groups have used the Internet to express their viewpoints, sell their paraphernalia, and recruit new members."[247(p927)] One study found that over two-thirds (67%) of young people between 15 and 18 years old have been exposed to hate material online and that one-fifth (21%) fell victim to the online hate material.[248] With respect to hate crime in general, the United States Department of Justice collates data and reports on cases of hate crime,[249] stating that "experts estimate an average of 250,000 hate crimes were committed each year between 2004 and 2015 in the United States. The majority of these were not reported to law enforcement."[250]

With its ubiquity, ease of use, and affordability, the internet has enabled people all over the world to connect with one another, for better or worse. The internet has allowed an audience for violence and hate via social media; for example, in May 2022, the perpetrator of the Uvalde school shooting threatened rape and homicide on social media the month before he committed mass murder of children.[251] From these, online hate groups have proliferated and are accessed by future perpetrators of violence and mass shootings. A sample of the deadly results when online hatred goes offline:

> White supremacist Wade Michael Page posted in online forums tied to hate before he went on to murder six people at a Sikh temple in Wisconsin in 2012. Prosecutors said Dylann Roof 'self-radicalized' online before he murdered nine people at a black church in South Carolina in 2015. Robert Bowers, accused of murdering 11 elderly worshipers at a Pennsylvania synagogue in October [2018], had been active on Gab, a Twitter-like site used by white supremacists . . . a 30-year-old D.C. man who described himself as a white nationalist was arrested on a gun charge after concerned relatives alerted police to his violent outbursts, including saying that the victims at the synagogue 'deserved it.' Police say the man was online friends with Bowers.[252]

Online hate groups encourage interest in violence, weapons, and guns, all falling under the category of violence-defining risk factors. Moreover, they provide a group of individuals who encourage these pursuits actively and therefore encourage belief that violence is a socially acceptable choice.

However, not only has the internet facilitated hate groups, but it has enabled violent perpetrators to access technology to boast about their violence through live streaming. A gunman killed 51 Muslim worshippers at two different mosques in Christchurch, New Zealand, and livestreamed the mass murder on the internet.[251] Similarly, in May 2022, a shooter slaughtered 10 Black people in a Buffalo, New York, supermarket, livestreamed the massacre, and posted racist online content.[253]

This technology enables an online audience to express hate and racism, which explicitly or implicitly provides behavioral reinforcement for engaging in violence.

A related risk factor that falls under this category concerns other groups that do not necessarily espouse ideologies of hate but nevertheless similarly encourage individuals and members to engage in violence or criminal activity. While online hate groups have proliferated, gang membership has also increased in the United States: Gangs similarly provide a social mode of encouraging violence as an acceptable choice. Indeed, commentators have noted that being a member of a gang or hate group can foster this belief and have indicated that online hate groups are the cyberspace equivalent of street gangs.[254] Both foster peer groups that encourage hatred and violence. And like online hate groups, gang activity has also been linked to social media, including images posted by youth who mention gang associations on Twitter.[255]

The Department of Justice reported in 2015 that street gang membership had increased in about half (49%) the US jurisdictions surveyed, stayed the same in 43%, and decreased in only 8%. The same report found that prison gang membership increased in the previous two years.[256] According to the United Nations, between 2000 and 2017, over one million deaths were attributable to organized crime killings, defined as homicide committed in the context of gang violence or organized crime and homicide committed while engaging in other criminal acts (e.g., robbery and sexual assault).[127] The United Nations indicated that globally, this figure on homicide from organized crime groups was greater than the number of people killed from armed conflict.

On an interventional level, scholars have written for some time about successful approaches to gang violence prevention.[257] A review of the literature summarizes that "gang activity prevention focuses on disrupting the antisocial behaviors of gangs to reduce their overall harm to the community (e.g., civil gang injunctions, crime prevention through environmental design). Gang activity suppression programs are often deterrence-based and follow the 'pulling levers strategy' emphasizing arrest and imprisonment through targeted police and prosecution provisions . . . programs attempt to minimize future levels of gang violence and victimization by reducing gang member participation with the group."[258(p2)] Given increasing rates of gang membership,[256] continued research investment in sharpening these strategies seems warranted. Lessons learned from those efforts could be used to curb the influence of other organizations encouraging violence, such as deterring online hate groups from recruiting new members.

On a policy level, the United States Department of Justice recommends general steps to curb influence of hate crimes more generally, including: (1) community policing; (2) law-enforcement community partnerships; (3) creating public awareness; (4) prioritizing hate crimes; (5) investing in training for officers and deputies; and (6) creating a special task force on hate crimes.[250] Rigorous scientific research continues to be needed to develop innovative policies, interventions, and laws for reducing violence stemming from these groups who, in today's world, actively use the internet and social media to recruit, build membership, and communicate messages of hate and violence.

One approach to blunt online reinforcement of violence through social media was taken by Prime Minister Jacinda Ardern of New Zealand in the wake of the 28-year-old gunman murdering 51 Muslim worshippers at two different Christchurch mosques and livestreaming the mass murder on the internet.[251] The prime minister refused to speak the gunman's name, which denied the shooter notoriety or any narcissistic thrill of fame and also limited his influence on copycat killers.[259]

In the wake of this tragedy, Prime Minister Ardern also launched a global initiative called Christchurch Call, whose mission to end online violent terrorist and extremist content led her to try to prevent the livestream video of the shooting from being broadcast by the Christchurch killer.[260] By 2021, over 50 countries signed on to the initiative as well as technology companies such as Twitter, Facebook, and Google. Specifically, the prime minister has called for world leaders and technology firms to better understand the social media algorithms driving content of online hate groups. Christchurch Call strives to achieve policy change aimed at improving safety and reducing violence-defining risk factors that enable, and in many cases even encourage, mass violence.

Conclusion

Prioritizing Stronger Risk Factors to Prevent Violence

On May 24, 2022, the second worst school shooting in United States history occurred in Uvalde, Texas, when 21 people were killed, including 19 children and 2 teachers. Within a day, and as if on cue, the news media, politicians, and many in the public openly blamed mental illness for the massacre, classifying the shooter as a madman and asserting that the perpetrator had a "mental health challenge."[261] There has not been a shred of evidence to support these claims about mental illness or mental health problems. There has been no evidence to support these claims, even at the time of this writing, months after the tragedy. Notice how, on top of lack of evidence, language is used to reinforce the very elements of social stigma discussed earlier in the book, separating "us" from "them."

In fact, the actual, solid evidence currently available at the time of this writing is as follows: the perpetrator was young, male, owned two AR-style rifles, purchased 375 rounds of ammunition, was a high school dropout, had a history of antisocial behavior, made threats to rape, kidnap, and murder people, and at the time of his violence—as well as for months beforehand—shared his hatred, lack of empathy, homicidal ideation, and psychopathic rage with an audience online.[262,263] Sort these factors into the 3-Category Model of Violence, and one soon sees multiple risk factors, especially violence-defining risk factors, contributing to this heinous act leading to the death of 19 elementary school children between the ages of 9 and 11. Automatically blaming violence on mental illness diverts attention from these stronger risk factors society ought to prioritize, further stigmatizes people with mental illness, and obstructs effective violence prevention. That is the central thesis of this book.

Many in the public assume there is a strong link between violence and mental illness,[69] which has become a go-to cause of extreme or mass violence. The media and politicians foster this exaggeration by regularly (and quickly) making such connections publicly after violent acts occur.[70] This perpetuates the stigmatizing of people with mental illness, who provide easy scapegoats to blame for the violence. Further, the need to satisfy the human craving for a fast, comforting answer for violence fuels this bias. Everyone wants to be safe, feel safe, and to quickly understand why a tragedy has occurred. Popular culture further reinforces this link with movies and television characters who engage in extreme violence that is attributable to mental illness.

It is important to recognize that the public will never know about most of the violent acts committed in the world: identifying a single cause of those that do become known is unsupported by science and ignores the multitude of causes and factors leading to violence. It is equally important to recognize that the "us versus them" dynamic regarding mental health and mental illness is also vastly exaggerated. Virtually everyone at some point in their lives will likely experience at least one diagnosable psychiatric, developmental, personality, neurological, intellectual, or cognitive disorder or disability, to say nothing of the physical illness and trauma that can lead to the above disorders. A crystal-clear divide between the people who do or do not have mental illness, then, is fiction. Certainly, everyone reading this book has experienced anger, which is shown to be a stronger and more consistent predictor of violence than mental illness.[23,30,134]

To counter social stigma and cognitive biases, we need to recognize "there is no basis for the public's generalized fear of people with mental illness. Having a psychiatric diagnosis is neither necessary nor sufficient as a risk factor for committing an act of mass violence."[66(pVI)] Mental illness is not irrelevant to violence risk but is less relevant than generally perceived: numerous other risk factors have stronger links to violence. Compared to other risk factors, mental health problems ranked low—and never fell in the top five—across multiple types of violence, including intimate partner homicide, targeted school violence, child sexual abuse, campus violence, intimate partner violence, mass attacks in public places, sexual violence/offenses, attacks on government officials and buildings, and stalking. Evidence shows that the public's view of mental illness as a top cause of violence is mistaken.

Exaggerations about the role of mental illness in violence distract us from attending to many other risk factors that play a major role. Put differently, overweighting of the role of mental illness means underweighting the more credible factors leading to violence, including antisocial personality disorder, criminal behavior, alcohol and drug abuse, anger, impulsivity, trauma, child abuse, financial strain, and unsafe neighborhoods, among other conditions and experiences.

Ultimately, the belief that mental illness and violence are strongly linked is not only unfounded but is itself dangerous: ignoring other stronger factors makes society less safe. While social stigma fueling a perceived dichotomy between people with and without mental illness may make some people feel better about themselves, by encouraging exaggerated beliefs in the role of mental illness in violence, it does little to make anyone safer. Zeroing in on mental illness as a single cause of violence will inevitably be limited because multiple causes of violence far more powerful than mental illness need to be addressed, particularly risk factors signaling that violence is an acceptable choice. This is consistent with recommendations from the USSS National Threat Assessment Center (NTAC): "While there is no sure way to predict human behavior or attribute violence to a single cause, early intervention is a demonstrated best practice for preventing unwanted behavior."[144(p27)]

As a result, there is a need to ensure that violence prevention addresses multiple risk factors. The 3-Category Violence Model helps one organize violence risk factors, like placing puzzle pieces into three different piles: external and internal risk factors as well as violence-defining risk factors. By focusing exclusively on mental illness, we only see a single puzzle piece in a single pile. This focus does not improve safety because it misses the opportunity to extend policies and other safeguards to all three categories, which would protect society and increase public safety, including the following ten strategies to prevent violence:

- Improving social environment and neighborhood
- Addressing and bolstering financial well-being
- Enhancing employment and work outcomes

- Building positive social support and curbing family violence
- Improving anger management and emotion regulation
- Treating substance abuse and mental illness
- Addressing trauma, abuse, and bullying
- Modifying criminal thinking and preventing antisocial behavior
- Promoting gun safety and safe storage of firearms
- Minimizing influence of groups encouraging hate and violence

Diverse approaches fall under the three risk-factor categories, ranging from addressing histories of trauma or abuse to promoting financial literacy and well-being to anger management therapy and interventions to help end substance abuse; also important are strategies that make violence seem less viable, including addressing hateful rhetoric on social media to promoting the safe storage of firearms. Each of these strategies requires increased research funding[264] to develop science-based approaches to interventions and policies, thus optimizing violence prevention in all 3 categories of risk factors. The third category, violence-defining risk factors, must be especially prioritized to prevent violence, including firearm safety research,[243] because these factors increase the risk of violence, define the violent act itself, and are among the strongest predictors of violence.

Another theme throughout this book is that violence is not only about the person but also about the environment, consistent with recommendations from the CDC.[157] Arguments that emphasize the person and not the environment when discussing violence are based on cognitive bias (the fundamental attribution error) and a false premise that a person lives in a vacuum. As stated throughout this book, behavior is a function of a person *and* their environment. To illustrate, in the 3-Category Violence Model, greater access to deadly weapons increases the viability of violence, the ease with which violent acts can be perpetrated. In turn, because access to weapons has been shown to be associated with increased risk of violence such as intimate partner homicide, we can logically infer that increased ease of perpetrating violence increases risk of violence in society at large, by definition. The point is that the environment, especially related to violence-defining factors, must be considered and prioritized in violence prevention policy.

As a result, while the health professions can address individual risk factors to some extent, the environment risk factors need to be addressed by scientifically informed policies and laws as well as by intelligence and law enforcement agencies. Even if clinicians had the power to predict and prevent every act of violence, they could only go so far: because mental illness is a weaker factor than perceived and because they are not equipped to modify large-scale environment violence risk factors.

So, although we do not delve into policy and law in detail, the responsibility nevertheless falls upon policymakers to allocate funds to improve neighborhoods, enhance financial literacy, increase employment, bolster positive social support, promote gun safety and education, and diminish the influence of hate groups. Even improving the ability to address individual factors relies on law and policy, such as funding research priorities to conduct randomized controlled trials of promising interventions to prevent violence (e.g., anger management, mindfulness, treatment of trauma symptoms and co-occurring mental illness and substance abuse).

While guns alone cannot be blamed for violence, their lethality and proliferation cannot be ignored or minimized. Laws and policies promoting secure gun storage are important for evaluating the impact of guns on public safety. Other policies and practices require more research to determine effectiveness in reducing violence. While guns occupy a unique place in our country's history, culture, and politics, they should be treated in a practical way that prioritizes safety while preserving citizens' rights to self-defense, hunting, and sport.

Broadcast media reporters, pundits, and politicians can do better. They can start by emphasizing what they do and do not know about a violent event and only add information as it is confirmed. Speculation should be kept to a minimum. The concept of causation by multiple factors should be explained and repeated, to prepare people to understand the factors when they are confirmed, and to dissuade people from wrongly settling on only one presumed cause. Highlighting or speculating on mental illness as "the" cause before any psychiatric history is definitely known ought to be considered unethical.

Conversely, the news media can strive to better balance reports of mental illness. Studies have shown that newspapers most often feature articles about mental illness in conjunction with a violent act,[57-59] often a sensationalistic editorial choice that too often leads readers to associate violence with mental illness. They are much less likely to report, for example, about the person who struggled with schizophrenia for 25 years and now runs a business. They are much less likely to report on the person with bipolar disorder working for the Peace Corps and helping impoverished children in other nations. They are much less likely to report on the person with major depression, now much improved, who was voted Teacher of the Year. For most people, then, the media exaggeration of violence and mental illness in society is pervasive and powerful. Media reinforcement of the link between mental illness and living a successful life is relatively sparse.

As citizens, we can do better too. A national survey conducted in 2021 revealed that 21% of US adults believed that threatening public health officials was justified, an increase from a year earlier when the figure was 15%.[265] As described many times in this book, the more people feel emboldened to think that violence is acceptable, the more likely it is that violence will occur. For this reason, discouraging others from believing that violent threats are justified would help promote peaceful and respectful discourse and reduce the risk of violence in society overall.

Members of the public can also stop instantaneously implicating mental illness as the cause of extreme violence. Instead of questioning whether mental illness is related to a violent event, we can "think slow" and instead consider what else might be involved by using the 3-Category Violence Model as a guide. What do we know about the situation and about the perpetrator? How did the perpetrator come to see violence as an acceptable option? What individual-level factors other than mental illness were at play? What kind of access did they have to weapons to complete the violent act? In what ways did the perpetrator show lack of empathy or concern for other human beings?

The biases we have widely come to embrace, emphasizing one or two risk factors rather than examining the many risk factors that contribute to the perpetration of violence, have made us less safe. In August 2019, the National Council for Behavioral Health issued a report entitled "Mass Violence in America: Causes, Impacts, and Solutions" and is clear about the multiple risk factors that contribute to the most heinous acts of violence: "Simplistic conclusions ignore the fact that mass violence is caused by many social and psychological factors that interact in complex ways."[66(pVI)] Among those social factors are environment-level variables that should not be discounted because they have established links to violence (e.g., gun access as the biggest risk factor in intimate partner homicide, with a very large effect size). It is time to recognize that there are many relevant, interacting factors at play and that violence is never the result of a single cause. This approach to thinking about risk factors of violence is rational, nuanced, and responsive rather than emotional, unitary, and reactive. It will require more attention, discipline, and commitment from politicians, media, law enforcement, medicine, psychology, social services, educators, and the public at large.

Nuance and complexity may not make for an exciting broadcast, but they do make for a truthful one. The solution to the violence puzzle recognizes there are complex sets of risk factors that fall into distinct categories. People who want quick, simple answers may criticize nuance as vague, indecisive, and difficult to achieve. But achieving it with respect to violence is literally a matter of life and death. Without recognizing all the causes of violence and prioritizing those with the strongest links to violence, the cycle of misunderstandings associated with violence and its prevention will continue unabated.

It is not only shortsighted but also dangerous for society to oversimplify the issue of violence. Just because internal or external risk factors such as poverty or mental illness may have been pertinent in a specific case of violence does not justify downplaying risk factors like antisocial personality disorder, psychopathic traits, and access to weapons. To solve the puzzle of violence, the multiple factors underlying violence need to be addressed, especially the violence-defining risk factors that are part of every single violent act. We should prioritize strategies for reducing the acceptability and viability of violence as a choice. Repeatedly blaming mental illness for violence will not make more powerful risk factors disappear. Instead, ignoring or downplaying stronger violence risk factors will lead to a more dangerous society, for us all.

ACKNOWLEDGMENTS

Many people contributed to this book. I want to thank the anonymous reviewers who provided extremely useful comments and Jennifer Hammer at NYU Press, whose superb advice helped shape the book's organization. A number of the ideas in this book originate from work on my dissertation in the University of Nebraska-Lincoln Law and Psychology Program, which is where I was encouraged to think scientifically about how people think about violence. I want to express gratitude for the opportunity over the years to have worked together on the subject matter of this book with Shannon Blakey, Stephanie Brooks Holliday, Sally Johnson, Mario Scalora, Shoba Sreenivasan, Jeffrey Swanson, Marvin Swartz, Richard Van Dorn, and Lynn Van Male, and to have had invaluable dialogue with experts in the field, including Paul Appelbaum, Kevin Douglas, Thomas Grisso, Stephen Hart, Kirk Heilbrun, John Monahan, and Jennifer Skeem. Our informative and enlightening discussions in the past two decades were critical to the writing of this book. Regarding feedback specific to the book, I would like to thank Lauren Kois, Cary Levine, and Ryan Wagner. These scholars provided vital insights into substantive aspects of the book, and following their excellent suggestions allowed the book's central thesis to be communicated concisely and more effectively. I would like to give a special thanks to Matthew Huss and Marc Patry, researchers in the field of law and psychology, for their support and help with this book, and most importantly, for their friendship and comradery. This book would not have been written if not for the mentorship of Jeannie Beckham and Alan Tomkins. They have served as role models of the highest integrity. I am incredibly grateful for all the guidance they have provided me throughout my career. I want to thank Nico for collaborating on this book. I very much valued the process of how our thought-provoking conversations inspired the evolution of ideas presented in this book. Finally, I thank my friends and family for their support, including Betsey, Chloe, Ethan, my parents, my siblings, and my in-laws. The literally thousands of times you helped uplift and motivate me while writing this book must be acknowledged. The depth of how much I appreciate (appreash) you and your encouragement cannot be understated. Thank you, beyond words.

EE

Thanks to my generous coauthor for inviting me to join him in writing this book. Thanks to my clients, who taught me what works and what does not. For their moral support and encouragement during the writing process, many thanks to Andrea, Joseph, and George Verykoukis; Tom Berger; Catherine Berger; Santiago and Mary Michaels Estrada; George and Nancy Soule; Neal Decker; and David Wynne.

NV

BIBLIOGRAPHY

1. Specia M, Khan AJ. Texas synagogue hostage taker had "mental health issues," brother in U.K. says. *New York Times*. January 17, 2022. https://web.archive.org /web/20220117214433/https://www.nytimes.com/2022/01/17/world/europe/texas -synagogue-hostage-taker-family.html. Accessed July 26, 2022.
2. Steinbuch Y. Texas synagogue hostage-taker had "mental health issues," brother says. *New York Post*. January 17, 2022. https://nypost.com/2022/01/17/texas -synagogue-hostage-taker-malik-faisal-akram-had-mental-health-issues-brother -says/. Accessed July 26, 2022.
3. Goldberg BT, Wolfe J. Texas synagogue hostage-taker was a British citizen; two arrested in England. *Reuters*. January 17, 2022. https://www.reuters.com/world/us /biden-calls-texas-synagogue-hostage-situation-act-terror-2022-01-16/. Accessed July 26, 2022.
4. Caldwell T, Vera A, Hanna J. New details emerge about hostage-taker's behavior in days before Texas synagogue standoff. *CNN*. January 20, 2022. https://www.cnn .com/2022/01/19/us/colleyville-texas-synagogue-investigation-wednesday/index .html. Accessed July 26, 2022.
5. Wallace D. Texas synagogue hostage suspect timeline: Malik Faisal Akram's criminal record and when he entered US. *Fox News*. January 19, 2022. https://www .foxnews.com/us/texas-synagogue-malik-faisal-akram-criminal-record. Accessed July 26, 2022.
6. Douglas J, Zapotosky M, Fisher M. Angry outbursts and cool determination: Inside the synagogue attacker's 18-day journey to terror. *Washington Post*. January 22, 2022. https://www.washingtonpost.com/politics/angry-outbursts-and -cool-determination-inside-the-synagogue-attackers-18-day-journey-to-terror /2022/01/22/2015da20-7931-11ec-83e1-eaef0fe4b8c9_story.html. Accessed July 26, 2022.
7. Fielding J, Robinson M. Moment synagogue terrorist was arrested outside his Blackburn home in 2018 after refusing to pay his landlord rent—as it's revealed he was dropped from UK terror watchlist months before siege. *Daily Mail*. January 18, 2022. https://www.dailymail.co.uk/news/article-10413273/British-terrorist -hunted-cops-days-flew-New-York.html. Accessed July 26, 2022.
8. Texas synagogue siege: British man who took four hostages in Colleyville "had been investigated by MI5." *Sky News*. January 18, 2022. https://news.sky.com/story /texas-synagogue-siege-british-man-who-took-four-hostage-in-colleyville-was -known-to-mi5-12519020. Accessed July 26, 2022.

9. Texas synagogue gunman was probed by UK's MI5 in 2020 as possible terror threat. *Times of Israel*. January 18, 2022. https://www.timesofisrael.com/texas -synagogue-gunman-was-probed-by-uks-mi5-in-2020-as-possible-terror-threat/. Accessed July 26, 2022.

10. Campbell J, Hanna J, Maxouris C. FBI is working to determine where Texas synagogue hostage-taker acquired his gun, official says. *CNN*. January 21, 2022. https: //www.cnn.com/2022/01/21/us/texas-synagogue-hostage-taker-death/index.html. Accessed July 26, 2022.

11. Harkay J, Hartley J, Ramirez D. Texas officials say all hostages safe, out of Colleyville synagogue; hostage-taker dead. *Fort Worth Star Telegram*. January 18, 2022. https://www.star-telegram.com/news/local/crime/article257360862.html. Accessed July 26, 2022.

12. Metzl JM, MacLeish KT. Mental illness, mass shootings, and the politics of American firearms. *Am J Public Health*. 2015;105(2):240–249. http://doi:10.2105/ AJPH.2014.302242.

13. American Psychiatric Association. *Diagnostic and Statistical Manual of Mental Disorders-Fifth Edition*. Arlington, VA: American Psychiatric Publishing; 2013.

14. Substance Abuse and Mental Health Services Administration. What are serious mental illnesses? https://www.samhsa.gov/serious-mental-illness. Accessed July 26, 2022.

15. Swanson JW, Holzer CE III, Ganju VK, Jono RT. Violence and psychiatric disorder in the community: evidence from the Epidemiologic Catchment Area surveys. *Hosp Community Psychiatry*. 1990;41(7):761–770. http://doi:10.1176/ps.41.7.761.

16. Fazel S, Gulati G, Linsell L, Geddes JR, Grann M. Schizophrenia and violence: systematic review and meta-analysis. *PLoS Med*. 2009;6(8):e1000120. http:// doi:10.1371/journal.pmed.1000120.

17. Skeem J, Mulvey E. What role does serious mental illness play in mass shootings, and how should we address it? *Criminol Public Policy*. 2020;19(1):85–108.

18. Appelbaum PS. Public safety, mental disorders, and guns. *JAMA Psychiatry*. 2013;70(6):565–566. http://doi:10.1001/jamapsychiatry.2013.315.

19. Thornicroft G. People with severe mental illness as the perpetrators and victims of violence: time for a new public health approach. *Lancet Public Health*. 2020;5(2):e72–e73. http://doi:10.1016/S2468–2667(20)30002–5.

20. Desmarais SL, Van Dorn RA, Johnson KL, Grimm KJ, Douglas KS, Swartz MS. Community violence perpetration and victimization among adults with mental illnesses. *Am J Public Health*. 2014;104(12):2342–2349. http://doi:10.2105/ AJPH.2013.301680.

21. Taylor PJ, Kalebic N. Psychosis and homicide. *Curr Opin Psychiatry*. May 2018;31(3):223–230. http://doi:10.1097/yco.0000000000000411.

22. Harford TC, Chen CM, Kerridge BT, Grant BF. Self- and other-directed forms of violence and their relationship with lifetime DSM-5 psychiatric disorders: results from the National Epidemiologic Survey on Alcohol Related Conditions-

III (NESARC-III). *Psychiatry Res.* 2018;262:384–392. http://doi:10.1016/j.psy chres.2017.09.012.

23. Elbogen EB, Dennis PA, Johnson SC. Beyond mental illness: targeting stronger and more direct pathways to violence. *Clin Psychol Sci.* 2016;4(5):747–759.

24. United States Census Bureau. New Vintage 2021 population estimates available for the nation, states and Puerto Rico. December 21, 2021. https://www.census.gov /newsroom/press-releases/2021/2021-population-estimates.html. Accessed July 26, 2022.

25. Pinker S. *The Better Angels of Our Nature: Why Violence Has Declined.* New York: Penguin; 2012.

26. National Institute of Mental Health. Mental health information: statistics. https: //www.nimh.nih.gov/health/statistics. Accessed July 26, 2022.

27. Hasin DS, Sarvet AL, Meyers JL, et al. Epidemiology of adult DSM-5 major depressive disorder and its specifiers in the United States. *JAMA Psychiatry.* 2018;75(4):336–346. http://doi:10.1001/jamapsychiatry.2017.4602.

28. Grant BF, Saha TD, Ruan WJ, et al. Epidemiology of DSM-5 drug use disorder: results from the National Epidemiologic Survey on Alcohol and Related Conditions–III. *JAMA Psychiatry.* 2016;73(1):39–47. http://doi:10.1001/jamapsychiatry.2015.2132.

29. Kuhns JB, Exum ML, Clodfelter TA, Bottia MC. The prevalence of alcohol-involved homicide offending: a meta-analytic review. *Homicide Stud.* 2013;18(3):251–270. http://doi:10.1177/1088767913493629.

30. Steadman HJ, Silver E, Monahan J, et al. A classification tree approach to the development of actuarial violence risk assessment tools. *Law Hum Behav.* 2000;24(1):83–100. http://doi:10.1023/a:1005478820425.

31. Goodwin RD, Hamilton SP. Lifetime comorbidity of antisocial personality disorder and anxiety disorders among adults in the community. *Psychiatry Res.* 2003;117(2):159–66. http://doi:10.1016/s0165-1781(02)00320-7.

32. Insel T. Transforming diagnosis. National Institute of Mental Health. April 29, 2013. http://psychrights.org/2013/130429NIMHTransformingDiagnosis.htm. Accessed July 26, 2022.

33. Frances A. *Saving Normal: An Insider's Revolt against Out-of-Control Psychiatric Diagnosis, DSM-5, Big Pharma, and the Medicalization of Ordinary Life.* New York: William Morrow & Co; 2013.

34. Frances A. Resuscitating the biopsychosocial model. *Lancet Psychiatry.* 2014;1(7):496–7. http://doi:10.1016/s2215-0366(14)00058-3.

35. Gask L. In defence of the biopsychosocial model. *Lancet Psychiatry.* 2018;5(7):548–549. http://doi:10.1016/S2215-0366(18)30165-2.

36. World Health Organization Commission on Social Determinants of Health. *Closing the Gap in a Generation: Health Equity through Action on the Social Determinants of Health: Commission on Social Determinants of Health Final Report.* Geneva, Switzerland: World Health Organization; 2008.

37. Allen J, Balfour R, Bell R, Marmot M. Social determinants of mental health. *Int Rev Psychiatry*. 2014;26(4):392–407. http://doi:10.3109/09540261.2014.928270.

38. Marmot M, Wilkinson R. *Social Determinants of Health*. Oxford: Oxford University Press; 2005.

39. Kandel ER. *The Disordered Mind: What Unusual Brains Tell Us about Ourselves*. New York: Farrar, Straus and Giroux; 2018.

40. Kandel E. The new science of mind and the future of knowledge. *Neuron*. 2013;80(3):546–560. https://doi.org/10.1016/j.neuron.2013.10.039.

41. Scull A. *Madness in Civilization*. Princeton, NJ: Princeton University Press; 2015.

42. Corrigan PW, Druss BG, Perlick DA. The impact of mental illness stigma on seeking and participating in mental health care. *Psychol Sci Public Interest*. 2014;15(2):37–70. http://doi:10.1177/1529100614531398.

43. Link BG, Phelan JC. Conceptualizing stigma. *Annu Rev Sociol*. 2001;27(1):363–385. http://doi:10.1146/annurev.soc.27.1.363.

44. Tajfel H, Turner, JC. The social identity theory of intergroup behavior. In: Jost JT, Sidanius J., eds. *Political Psychology: Key Readings*. London, UK: Psychology Press; 2004:276–293. https://doi.org/10.4324/9780203505984-16.

45. Tajfel H. Social identity and intergroup behaviour. *Soc Sci Inf*. 1974;13(2):65–93.

46. Nussbaum MC. *Upheavals of Thought: The Intelligence of Emotions*. Cambridge: Cambridge University Press; 2003.

47. Major B, O'Brien LT. The social psychology of stigma. *Annu Rev Psychol*. 2005;56:393–421. http://doi:10.1146/annurev.psych.56.091103.070137.

48. Kurzban R, Leary MR. Evolutionary origins of stigmatization: the functions of social exclusion. *Psychol Bull*. 2001;127(2):187–208. http://doi:10.1037/0033-2909.127.2.187.

49. Blanco W, Roberts JT. *Herodotus, The Histories*. Translated by Walter Blanco. New York: Norton; 1992.

50. *The Holy Bible, Revised Standard Version, Second Edition*. Nashville, TN: Thomas Nelson; 1971.

51. Nilsson MP. *Greek Popular Religion*. Vol 1. New York: Columbia University Press; 1940.

52. Riordan DV. Scapegoating mentally ill people. *Br J Psychiatry*. 2019;215(2):504–505. http://doi:10.1192/bjp.2019.148.

53. Saad L. Americans fault mental health system most for gun violence. *Gallup*. September 20, 2013. https://news.gallup.com/poll/164507/americans-fault-mental-health-system-gun-violence.aspx. Accessed July 26, 2022.

54. Monmouth University Polling Institute. Public disagrees with SCOTUS on guns. June 30, 2022. https://www.monmouth.edu/polling-institute/reports/monmouthpoll_us_063022/. Accessed July 26, 2022.

55. Sandy Hook Advisory Commission. Final report of the Sandy Hook advisory commission. February 2015. http://www.governor.ct.gov/malloy/lib/malloy/SHAC_Doc_2015.02.13_draft_version_of_final_report.pdf. Accessed July 31, 2022.

56. Burns M. Wake Forest man guilty of first degree murder in 2016 shooting death of neighbors. *WRAL.COM*. April 8, 2019. https://www.wral.com/wake-forest-man

-guilty-of-first-degree-murder-in-2016-shooting-deaths-of-neighbors/18313369/. Accessed July 26, 2022.

57. McGinty EE, Kennedy-Hendricks A, Choksy S, Barry CL. Trends in news media coverage of mental illness in the United States: 1995–2014. *Health Aff (Millwood).* 2016;35(6):1121–1129. http://doi:10.1377/hlthaff.2016.0011.

58. McGinty EE, Webster DW, Jarlenski M, Barry CL. News media framing of serious mental illness and gun violence in the United States, 1997–2012. *Am J Public Health.* 2014;104(3):406–413. http://doi:10.2105/AJPH.2013.301557.

59. Wahl OF. News media portrayal of mental illness: implications for public policy. *Am Behav Sci.* 2003;46(12):1594–1600.

60. Phillips S. The most dangerous deviants in America: why the disabled are depicted as deranged killers. In: Rubin LC. *Mental Illness in Popular Media: Essays on the Representation of Disorders.* Jefferson, NC: McFarland; 2012:64–76.

61. Wahl OF. *Media Madness: Public Images of Mental Illness.* New Brunswick, NJ: Rutgers University Press; 1995.

62. Smith DL. *Less Than Human: Why We Demean, Enslave, and Exterminate Others.* New York: St. Martin's Press; 2011.

63. Brauser D. Experts, patients decry Trump characterization of "mentally ill monsters" after mass shootings. *Medscape.* August 6, 2019. https://www.medscape.com/viewarticle/916475?reg = 1. Accessed July 26, 2022.

64. Haugen PT, McCrillis AM, Smid GE, Nijdam MJ. Mental health stigma and barriers to mental health care for first responders: a systematic review and meta-analysis. *J Psychiatr Res.* 2017;94:218–229. http://doi:10.1016/j.jpsychires.2017.08.001.

65. Corrigan P. How stigma interferes with mental health care. *Am Psychol.* 2004;59(7):614–625. http://doi:10.1037/0003-066X.59.7.614.

66. Parks J, Bechtold D, Shelp F, Lieberman J, Coffey S. Mass violence in America: causes, impacts and solutions. In: *National Council on Mental Wellbeing.* National Council; 2019. https://www.thenationalcouncil.org/resources/mass-violence-in-america-causes-impacts-and-solutions/.

67. Pasewark RA, Seidenzahl D. Opinions concerning the insanity plea and criminality among mental patients. *Bull Am Acad Psychiatry Law.* 1979;7(2):199–204.

68. Silver E, Cirincione C, Steadman HJ. Demythologizing inaccurate perceptions of the insanity defense. *Law Hum Behav.* 1994;18(1):63–70.

69. Pescosolido BA, Manago B, Monahan J. Evolving public views on the likelihood of violence from people with mental illness: stigma and its consequences. *Health Aff (Millwood).* 2019;38(10):1735–1743. http://doi:10.1377/hlthaff.2019.00702.

70. Gold LH. *Gun Violence and Mental Illness.* Washington, DC: American Psychiatric Association; 2015.

71. Kahneman D. *Thinking, Fast and Slow.* New York: Macmillan; 2011.

72. Corrigan PW, Kleinlein P. The impact of mental illness stigma. In: Corrigan PW, *On the Stigma of Mental Illness: Practical Strategies for Research and Social Change.* Washington, DC: American Psychological Association; 2005:11–44.

73. Chapman LJ, Chapman JP. Illusory correlation as an obstacle to the use of valid psychodiagnostic signs. *J Abnorm Psychol.* 1969;74(3):271–280. http://doi:10.1037/h0027592.

74. Elbogen EB, Huss MT, Tomkins AJ, Scalora MJ. Clinical decision making about psychopathy and violence risk assessment in public sector mental health settings. *Psychol Serv.* 2005;2(2):133.

75. Brown B, Rakow T. Understanding clinicians' use of cues when assessing the future risk of violence: a clinical judgement analysis in the psychiatric setting. *Clin Psychol Psychother.* 2016;23(2):125–141. http://doi:10.1002/cpp.1941.

76. Elbogen EB. The process of violence risk assessment: a review of descriptive research. *Aggress Violent Behav,* 2002; 7(6): 591–604. https://doi.org/10.1016/S1359-1789(01)00051-9.

77. Quinsey VL. The prediction and explanation of criminal violence. *Int J Law Psychiatry.* 1995;18(2):117–127.

78. Lewin K. Behavior and development as a function of the total situation. In: Carmichel L. *Manual of Child Psychology.* John Wiley & Sons; 1946:791–844.

79. Lewin K. *Principles Of Topological Psychology.* McGraw-Hill; 1936.

80. Silver E. Race, neighborhood disadvantage, and violence among persons with mental disorders: the importance of contextual measurement. *Law Hum Behav.* 2000;24(4):449–456. http://doi:10.1023/a:1005544330132.

81. Swanson JW, Swartz MS, Essock SM, et al. The social-environmental context of violent behavior in persons treated for severe mental illness. *Am J Public Health.* 2002;92(9):1523–1531. http://doi:10.2105/ajph.92.9.1523.

82. Spencer CM, Stith SM. Risk factors for male perpetration and female victimization of intimate partner homicide: a meta-analysis. *Trauma Violence Abuse.* 2020;21(3):527–540. http://doi:10.1177/1524838018781101.

83. Silver E, Teasdale B. Mental disorder and violence: an examination of stressful life events and impaired social support. *Soc Probl.* 2005;52(1):62–78.

84. Sturidsson K, Haggård-Grann U, Lotterberg M, Dernevik M, et al.. Clinicians' perceptions of which factors increase or decrease the risk of violence among forensic out-patients. *Int J Forensic Ment Health.* 2004;3(1):23–36.

85. Odeh MS, Zeiss RA, Huss MT. Cues they use: clinicians' endorsement of risk cues in predictions of dangerousness. *Behav Sci Law.* 2006;24(2):147–156. http://doi:10.1002/bsl.672.

86. Yelderman LA, Miller MK, Forsythe S, Sicafuse L. Understanding crime control theater: do sample type, gender, and emotions relate to support for crime control theater policies? *Crim Justice Rev.* 2018;43(2):147–173.

87. Mossman D. Assessing predictions of violence: being accurate about accuracy. *J Consult Clin Psychol.* 1994;62(4):783–792. http://doi:10.1037//0022-006x.62.4.783.

88. Heilbrun, Kirk. *Evaluation for Risk of Violence in Adults.* New York: Oxford University Press; 2009.

89. Fazel S, Burghart M, Fanshawe T, Gil SD, Monahan J, Yu R. The predictive performance of criminal risk assessment tools used at sentencing: systematic review of validation studies. *J Crim Justice*. 2022;81:101902.
90. Elbogen E. The process and context of violence risk assessment. In: Singh JP, Bjørkly S, Fazel S. *International Perspectives on Violence Risk Assessment*. Oxford: Oxford University Press; 2016: 53–75. https://doi.org/10.1093/acprof:oso /9780199386291.003.0005.
91. Murrie DC, Boccaccini MT, Guarnera LA, Rufino KA. Are forensic experts biased by the side that retained them? *Psychol Sci*. 2013;24(10):1889–1897. http:// doi:10.1177/0956797613481812.
92. Swanson JW, Swartz MS, Van Dorn RA, et al. Comparison of antipsychotic medication effects on reducing violence in people with schizophrenia. *Br J Psychiatry*. 2008;193(1):37–43. http://doi:10.1192/bjp.bp.107.042630.
93. Douglas KS, Skeem JL. Violence risk assessment: getting specific about being dynamic. *Psychol Public Policy Law*. 2005;11(3):347–383. http://doi:10.1037/1076–8971.11.3.347.
94. Levine TR, Serota KB, Shulman HC. The impact of lie to me on viewers' actual ability to detect deception. *Commun Res*. 2010;37(6):847–856. http://doi:10 .1177/0093650210362686.
95. Synnott J, Dietzel D, Ioannou M. A review of the polygraph: history, methodology and current status. *Crime Psychology Review*. 2015;1(1):59–83.
96. Iacono WG, Ben-Shakhar G. Current status of forensic lie detection with the comparison question technique: an update of the 2003 National Academy of Sciences report on polygraph testing. *Law Hum Behav*. 2019;43(1):86–98. http:// doi:10.1037/lhb0000307.
97. Skeem JL, Manchak SM, Lidz CW, Mulvey EP. The utility of patients' self-perceptions of violence risk: consider asking the person who may know best. *Psychiatr Serv*. 2013;64(5):410–415. http://doi:10.1176/appi.ps.001312012.
98. Grisso T, Davis J, Vesselinov R, Appelbaum PS, Monahan J. Violent thoughts and violent behavior following hospitalization for mental disorder. *J Consult Clin Psychol*. 2000;68(3):388–398.
99. Steadman HJ, Mulvey EP, Monahan J, et al. Violence by people discharged from acute psychiatric inpatient facilities and by others in the same neighborhoods. *Arch Gen Psychiatry*. 1998;55(5):393–401. http://doi:10.1001/archpsyc.55.5.393.
100. Whiting D, Lichtenstein P, Fazel S. Violence and mental disorders: a structured review of associations by individual diagnoses, risk factors, and risk assessment. *Lancet Psychiatry*. 2021;8(2):150–161. http://doi:10.1016/S2215-0366(20)30262-5.
101. Hammerton G, Munafò MR. Causal inference with observational data: the need for triangulation of evidence. *Psychol Med*. 2021;51(4):563–578. http://doi:10.1017 /S0033291720005127.
102. Parascandola M, Weed DL. Causation in epidemiology. *J Epidemiol Community Health*. 2001;55(12):905–912. http://doi:10.1136/jech.55.12.905.

103. Hill AB. The environment and disease: association or causation? 1965. *J R Soc Med*. 2015;108(1):32–37. http://doi:10.1177/0141076814562718.

104. Silver E, Mulvey EP, Swanson JW. Neighborhood structural characteristics and mental disorder: Faris and Dunham revisited. *Soc Sci Med*. 2002;55(8):1457–1470. http://doi:10.1016/s0277-9536(01)00266-0.

105. Aneshensel CS. Social stress: theory and research. *Annu Rev Sociol*. 1992;18(1):15–38.

106. Monahan J, Steadman HJ, Appelbaum PS, et al. Developing a clinically useful actuarial tool for assessing violence risk. *Br J Psychiatry*. 2000;176:312–319. http://doi:10.1192/bjp.176.4.312.

107. Monahan J, Steadman HJ, Robbins PC, et al. An actuarial model of violence risk assessment for persons with mental disorders. *Psychiatr Serv*. 2005;56(7):810–5. http://doi:10.1176/appi.ps.56.7.810.

108. Mulvey EP, Shaw E, Lidz CW. Why use multiple sources in research on patient violence in the community. *Crim Behav Ment Health*. 1994; 4(4):253–258.

109. Appelbaum PS, Robbins PC, Monahan J. Violence and delusions: data from the MacArthur Violence Risk Assessment Study. *Am J Psychiatry*. 2000;157(4):566–572. http://doi:10.1176/appi.ajp.157.4.566.

110. Skeem J, Kennealy P, Monahan J, Peterson J, Appelbaum P. Psychosis uncommonly and inconsistently precedes violence among high-risk individuals. *Clin Psychol Sci*. 2016;4(1):40–49.

111. Elbogen EB, Johnson SC. The intricate link between violence and mental disorder: results from the National Epidemiologic Survey on Alcohol and Related Conditions. *Arch Gen Psychiatry*. 2009;66(2):152–61. http://doi:10.1001/archgenpsychiatry.2008.537.

112. Van Dorn R, Volavka J, Johnson N. Mental disorder and violence: is there a relationship beyond substance use? *Soc Psychiatry Psychiatr Epidemiol*. 2012;47(3):487–503. http://doi:10.1007/s00127-011-0356-x.

113. Hasin DS, Grant BF. The National Epidemiologic Survey on Alcohol and Related Conditions (NESARC) Waves 1 and 2: review and summary of findings. *Soc Psychiatry Psychiatr Epidemiol*. 2015;50(11):1609–1640. doi:10.1007/s00127-015-1088-0.

114. Blakey SM, Love H, Lindquist L, Beckham JC, Elbogen EB. Disentangling the link between posttraumatic stress disorder and violent behavior: findings from a nationally representative sample. *J Consult Clin Psychol*. 2018;86(2):169–178. http://doi:10.1037/ccp0000253.

115. Fazel S, Lichtenstein P, Grann M, Goodwin GM, Långström N. Bipolar disorder and violent crime: new evidence from population-based longitudinal studies and systematic review. *Arch Gen Psychiatry*. 2010;67(9):931–8. http://doi:10.1001/archgenpsychiatry.2010.97.

116. Amrhein V, Greenland S, McShane B. Scientists rise up against statistical significance. *Nature*. 2019;567(7748):305–307. http://doi:10.1038/d41586-019-00857-9.

117. Ferguson CJ. *An Effect Size Primer: A Guide for Clinicians and Researchers: Methodological Issues and Strategies in Clinical Research*, 4th ed. Washington, DC: American Psychological Association; 2016:301–310.

118. Fazel S, Smith EN, Chang Z, Geddes JR. Risk factors for interpersonal violence: an umbrella review of meta-analyses. *Br J Psychiatry*. 2018;213(4):609–614. http://doi:10.1192/bjp.2018.145.

119. Whiting D, Gulati G, Geddes JR, Fazel S. Association of schizophrenia spectrum disorders and violence perpetration in adults and adolescents from 15 countries: a systematic review and meta-analysis. *JAMA Psychiatry*. 2022;79(2):120–132. http://doi:10.1001/jamapsychiatry.2021.3721.

120. Douglas KS, Guy LS, Hart SD. Psychosis as a risk factor for violence to others: a meta-analysis. *Psychol Bull*. 2009;135(5):679–706. http://doi:10.1037/a0016311.

121. Rice ME, Harris GT. Comparing effect sizes in follow-up studies: ROC Area, Cohen's d, and r. *Law Hum Behav*. 2005;29(5):615–620. http://doi:10.1007/s10979-005-6832-7.

122. Cohen J. *Statistical Power Analysis for the Behavioral Sciences (2nd Edition)*. New York: Routledge; 1988.

123. Douglas KS, Hart SD, Webster CD, Belfrage H, Guy LS, Wilson CM. Historical-clinical-risk management-20, Version 3 (HCR-20V3): development and overview. *Int J Forensic Ment Health*. 2014;13(2):93–108. http://doi:10.1080/14999013.2014.906519.

124. Stöckl H, Devries K, Rotstein A, et al. The global prevalence of intimate partner homicide: a systematic review. *Lancet*. 2013;382(9895):859–865. http://doi:10.1016/S0140-6736(13)61030-2.

125. Morgan RE, Thompson A. Criminal victimization, 2020—supplemental statistical tables. Bureau of Justice Statistics. https://bjs.ojp.gov/content/pub/pdf/cv20sst.pdf. Accessed July 26, 2022.

126. Petrosky E, Blair JM, Betz CJ, Fowler KA, Jack SPD, Lyons BH. Racial and ethnic differences in homicides of adult women and the role of intimate partner violence—United States, 2003–2014. *MMWR Morb Mortal Wkly Rep*. 2017;66(28):741–746. http://doi:10.15585/mmwr.mm6628a1.

127. United Nations Office on Drugs and Crime. Global study on homicide: homicide trends, patterns and criminal justice response. New York: United Nations; 2019. https://www.unodc.org/unodc/en/data-and-analysis/global-study-on-homicide.html. Accessed July 27, 2022.

128. Snyder RL. *No Visible Bruises: What We Don't Know about Domestic Violence Can Kill Us*. London: Bloomsbury; 2019.

129. United States Secret Service National Threat Assessment Center. *Mass Attacks in Public Spaces—2018*. Washington, DC: United States Secret Service National Threat Assessment Center; 2019. https://www.secretservice.gov/sites/default/files/2020-04/USSS_FY2019_MAPS.pdf. Accessed July 31, 2022.

130. Kivisto AJ, Porter M. Firearm use increases risk of multiple victims in domestic homicides. *J Am Acad Psychiatry Law*. 2020;48(1):26–34. http://doi:10.29158/JAAPL.003888–20.

131. Gold LH. Domestic violence, firearms, and mass shootings. *J Am Acad Psychiatry Law*. 2020;48(1):35–42. http://doi:10.29158/JAAPL.003929–20.

132. Kivisto AJ, Magee LA, Phalen PL, Ray BR. Firearm ownership and domestic versus nondomestic homicide in the US. *Am J Prev Med*. 2019;57(3):311–320. http://doi:10.1016/j.amepre.2019.04.009.

133. Calhoun FS, Weston SW. *Contemporary Threat Management: A Practical Guide for Identifying, Assessing, and Managing Individuals of Violent Intent*. San Diego, CA: Specialized Training Services; 2003.

134. Stith SM, Smith DB, Penn CE, Ward DB, Tritt D. Intimate partner physical abuse perpetration and victimization risk factors: a meta-analytic review. *Aggress Violent Behav*. 2004;10(1):65–98. https://doi.org/10.1016/j.avb.2003.09.001.

135. Smith SG, Zhang X, Basile KC, et al. The national intimate partner and sexual violence survey: 2015 data brief–updated release. Atlanta, GA: National Center for Injury Prevention Centers for Disease Control and Prevention; 2018. https://www.cdc.gov/violenceprevention/pdf/2015data-brief508.pdf.

136. Hanson RK, Morton-Bourgon KE. The characteristics of persistent sexual offenders: a meta-analysis of recidivism studies. *J Consult Clin Psychol*. 2005;73(6):1154–1163. http://doi:10.1037/0022–006X.73.6.1154.

137. Basile KC, Swahn MH, Chen J, Saltzman LE. Stalking in the United States: recent national prevalence estimates. *Am J Prev Med*. 2006;31(2):172–175. http://doi:10.1016/j.amepre.2006.03.028.

138. Rosenfeld B. Violence risk factors in stalking and obsessional harassment: a review and preliminary meta-analysis. *Crim Justice Behav*. 2004;31(1):9–36.

139. US Centers for Disease Control and Prevention. *What Is Child Sexual Abuse?* Washington, DC: CDC. https://www.cdc.gov/violenceprevention/childsexualabuse/fastfact.html. Accessed July 26, 2022.

140. Whitaker DJ, Le B, Karl Hanson R, et al. Risk factors for the perpetration of child sexual abuse: a review and meta-analysis. *Child Abuse Negl*. 2008;32(5):529–548. http://doi:10.1016/j.chiabu.2007.08.005.

141. Alathari L, Drysdale D, Driscoll S, et al. Protecting America's schools: a US Secret Service analysis of targeted school violence. Washington, DC: National Threat Assessment Center, 2019. https://www.secretservice.gov/sites/default/files/2020-04/Protecting_Americas_Schools.pdf. Accessed July 31, 2022.

142. Drysdale D, Modzeleski W, Simons A. *Campus Attacks: Targeted Violence Affecting Institutions of Higher Education*. US Secret Service, US Department of Homeland Security, Office of Safe and Drug-Free Schools, US Department of Education, and Federal Bureau of Investigation, US Department of Justice.; 2010.

143. United States Secret Service National Threat Assessment Center. *Attacks on Federal Government 2001–2013: Threat Assessment Considerations*. Washington,

DC: United States Secret Service National Threat Assessment Center; 2015. https://www.secretservice.gov/sites/default/files/2020-04/Attacks_on_Federal _Government_2001-2013.pdf. Accessed July 31, 2022.

144. United States Secret Service National Threat Assessment Center. *Mass Attacks in Public Spaces—2019*. Washington, DC: United States Secret Service National Threat Assessment Center; 2020. https://www.secretservice.gov/sites/default/files /reports/2020-09/MAPS2019.pdf. Accessed July 31, 2022.

145. Vlahovicova K, Melendez-Torres GJ, Leijten P, Knerr W, Gardner F. Parenting programs for the prevention of child physical abuse recurrence: a systematic review and meta-analysis. *Clin Child Fam Psychol Rev*. 2017;20(3):351–365. http:// doi:10.1007/s10567-017-0232-7.

146. Douglas KS, Ogloff JR, Nicholls TL, Grant I. Assessing risk for violence among psychiatric patients: the HCR-20 violence risk assessment scheme and the psychopathy checklist: screening version. *J Consult Clin Psychol*. 1999;67(6):917–930. http://doi:10.1037//0022-006x.67.6.917.

147. Salekin RT, Rogers R, Sewell KW. A review and meta-analysis of the psychopathy checklist and psychopathy checklist—revised: predictive validity of dangerousness. *Clin Psychol*. 1996;3(3):203.

148. Denson TF, DeWall CN, Finkel EJ. Self-control and aggression. *Curr Dir Psychol Sci*. 2012;21(1):20–25. http://doi:10.1177/0963721411429451.

149. DeWall CN, Finkel EJ, Denson TF. Self-control inhibits aggression. *Soc Personal Psychol Compass*. 2011;5(7):458–472.

150. Finkel EJ. The I³ model: metatheory, theory, and evidence. *Adv Exp Soc Psychol*. 2013;49:1.

151. Finkel EJ, DeWall CN, Slotter EB, McNulty JK, Pond RS Jr, Atkins DC. Using I³ theory to clarify when dispositional aggressiveness predicts intimate partner violence perpetration. *J Pers Soc Psychol*. 2012;102(3):533–549. http://doi:10.1037/a0025651.

152. Li JB, Nie YG, Boardley ID, Dou K, Situ QM. When do normative beliefs about aggression predict aggressive behavior? An application of I³ theory. *Aggress Behav*. 2015;41(6):544–555. http://doi:10.1002/ab.21594.

153. Slotter EB, Finkel EJ. I³ theory: instigating, impelling, and inhibiting factors in aggression. In: Shaver PR, Mikulincer M, eds. *Human Aggression and Violence: Causes, Manifestations, and Consequences*. Washington, DC: American Psychological Association; 2011:35–52.

154. Finkel EJ. Impelling and inhibiting forces in the perpetration of intimate partner violence. *Rev Gen Psychol*. 2007;11(2):193–207. http://doi:10.1037/1089-2680.11.2.193.

155. Slotter EB, Finkel EJ, Dewall CN, et al. Putting the brakes on aggression toward a romantic partner: the inhibitory influence of relationship commitment. *J Pers Soc Psychol*. 2012;102(2):291–305. http://doi:10.1037/a0024915.

156. Coleman R. Adam Lanza: timeline. https://schoolshooters.info/sites/default/files /lanza_timeline_1.0_1.pdf. Accessed July 31, 2022.

157. US Centers for Disease Control and Prevention. Risk and protective factors for perpetration. https://www.cdc.gov/violenceprevention/intimatepartnerviolence/riskprotectivefactors.html. Accessed July 26, 2022.

158. Kondo MC, Andreyeva E, South EC, MacDonald JM, Branas CC. Neighborhood interventions to reduce violence. *Annu Rev Public Health*. 2018;39:253–271. http://doi:10.1146/annurev-publhealth-040617-014600.

159. Hiday VA. The social context of mental illness and violence. *J Health Soc Behav*. 1995;36(2):122–137.

160. Cerdá M, Diez-Roux AV, Tchetgen ET, Gordon-Larsen P, Kiefe C. The relationship between neighborhood poverty and alcohol use: estimation by marginal structural models. *Epidemiology*. 2010;21(4):482–489. http://doi:10.1097/EDE.0b013e3181e13539.

161. Chauhan P, Widom CS. Childhood maltreatment and illicit drug use in middle adulthood: the role of neighborhood characteristics. *Dev Psychopathol*. 2012;24(3):723–738. http://doi:10.1017/S0954579412000338.

162. Branas CC, South E, Kondo MC, et al. Citywide cluster randomized trial to restore blighted vacant land and its effects on violence, crime, and fear. *Proc Natl Acad Sci U S A*. 2018;115(12):2946–2951. http://doi:10.1073/pnas.1718503115.

163. South EC, MacDonald J, Reina V. Association between structural housing repairs for low-income homeowners and neighborhood crime. *JAMA Network Open*. 2021;4(7):e2117067-e2117067. http://doi:10.1001/jamanetworkopen.2021.17067.

164. Gibson M, Hearty W, Craig P. The public health effects of interventions similar to basic income: a scoping review. *Lancet Public Health*. 2020;5(3):e165–e176. http://doi:10.1016/S2468-2667(20)30005-0.

165. Brück T, Ferguson NT, Izzi V, Stojetz W. Can jobs programs build peace? *World Bank Res Obs*. 2021;36(2):234–259.

166. Costello EJ, Compton SN, Keeler G, Angold A. Relationships between poverty and psychopathology: a natural experiment. *JAMA*. 2003;290(15):2023–2029. http://doi:10.1001/jama.290.15.2023.

167. Peverill M, Dirks MA, Narvaja T, Herts KL, Comer JS, McLaughlin KA. Socioeconomic status and child psychopathology in the United States: a meta-analysis of population-based studies. *Clin Psychol Rev*. 2021;83:101933. http://doi:10.1016/j.cpr.2020.101933.

168. Fernandes D, Lynch Jr JG, Netemeyer RG. Financial literacy, financial education, and downstream financial behaviors. *Manage Sci*. 2014;60(8):1861–1883.

169. Peeters N, Rijk K, Soetens B, Storms B, Hermans K. A systematic literature review to identify successful elements for financial education and counseling in groups. *J Consum Aff*. 2018;52(2):415–440.

170. Lusardi A, Mitchelli O. Financial literacy and retirement preparedness: evidence and implications for financial education. *Bus Econ*. 2007; 42:35–44. https://doi.org/10.2145/20070104

171. Hershfield HE, Goldstein DG, Sharpe WF, et al. Increasing saving behavior through age-progressed renderings of the future self. *J Mark Res.*
2011;48(SPL):S23-S37.

172. Davydenko M, Kolbuszewska M, Peetz J. A meta-analysis of financial self-control
strategies: comparing empirical findings with online media and lay person
perspectives on what helps individuals curb spending and start saving. *PLoS One.*
2021;16(7):e0253938. http://doi:10.1371/journal.pone.0253938.

173. Wyatt R, Anderson-Drevs K, Van Male LM. Workplace violence in health care:
a critical issue with a promising solution. *JAMA.* 2016;316(10):1037-1038. http://
doi:10.1001/jama.2016.10384.

174. Heller SB. Summer jobs reduce violence among disadvantaged youth. *Science.*
2014;346(6214):1219-1223. http://doi:10.1126/science.1257809.

175. Carr A. Family therapy and systemic interventions for child-focused problems:
the current evidence base. *J Fam Ther.* 2019;41(2):153-213.

176. Carr A. Couple therapy, family therapy and systemic interventions for
adult-focused problems: the current evidence base. *J Fam Ther.* 2019;41(4):
492-536.

177. Chiesa AE, Kallechey L, Harlaar N, et al. Intimate partner violence victimization
and parenting: a systematic review. *Child Abuse Negl.* 2018;80:285-300. http://
doi:10.1016/j.chiabu.2018.03.028.

178. Karakurt G, Koç E, Çetinsaya EE, Ayluçtarhan Z, Bolen S. Meta-analysis and
systematic review for the treatment of perpetrators of intimate partner violence. *Neurosci Biobehav Rev.* 2019;105:220-230. http://doi:10.1016/j.neubio-
rev.2019.08.006.

179. Karakurt G, Whiting K, Esch C, Bolen SD, Calabrese JR. Couples therapy for
intimate partner violence: a systematic review and meta-analysis. *J Marital Fam
Ther.* 2016;42(4):567-583. http://doi:10.1111/jmft.12178.

180. Santirso FA, Gilchrist G, Lila M, Gracia E. Motivational strategies in interventions
for intimate partner violence offenders: a systematic review and meta-analysis
of randomized controlled trials. *Interv Psicosoc.* 2020;29(3):175-190. http://
doi:10.5093/pi2020a13.

181. Stephens-Lewis D, Johnson A, Huntley A, et al. Interventions to reduce intimate
partner violence perpetration by men who use substances: a systematic review
and meta-analysis of efficacy. *Trauma Violence Abuse.* 2021;22(5):1262-1278. http://
doi:10.1177/1524838019882357.

182. Travers Á, McDonagh T, Cunningham T, Armour C, Hansen M. The effectiveness of interventions to prevent recidivism in perpetrators of intimate partner
violence: a systematic review and meta-analysis. *Clin Psychol Rev.* 2021;84:101974.
http://doi:10.1016/j.cpr.2021.101974.

183. Reynolds AJ, Temple JA, Ou SR, et al. Effects of a school-based, early childhood
intervention on adult health and well-being: a 19-year follow-up of low-income
families. *Arch Pediatr Adolesc Med.* 2007;161(8):730-739. http://doi:10.1001/arch-
pedi.161.8.730.

184. Branas CC, Reeping PM, Rudolph KE. Beyond gun laws-innovative interventions to reduce gun violence in the United States. *JAMA Psychiatry*. 2021;78(3):243–244. http://doi:10.1001/jamapsychiatry.2020.2493.

185. Del Vecchio T, O'Leary KD. Effectiveness of anger treatments for specific anger problems: a meta-analytic review. *Clin Psychol Rev*. 2004;24(1):15–34. http://doi:10.1016/j.cpr.2003.09.006.

186. Saini M. A meta-analysis of the psychological treatment of anger: developing guidelines for evidence-based practice. *J Am Acad Psychiatry Law*. 2009;37(4):473–488.

187. Reilly PM, Shopshire MS. *Anger Management for Substance Abuse and Mental Health Clients: Cognitive Behavioral Therapy Manual*. Washington, DC: US Department of Health & Human Services; 2019. https://store.samhsa.gov/product /Anger-Management-for-Substance-Abuse-and-Mental-Health-Clients-A -Cognitive-Behavioral-Therapy-Manual/PEP19-02-01-001.

188. American Psychological Assessment. Understanding anger: how psychologists help with anger problems. Washington, DC: American Psychological Association; 2017. https://www.apa.org/topics/anger/understanding. Accessed July 26, 2022.

189. Lee AH, DiGiuseppe R. Anger and aggression treatments: a review of meta-analyses. *Curr Opin Psychol*. Feb 2018;19:65–74. http://doi:10.1016/j.copsyc.2017.04.004.

190. Sammut Henwood K, Chou S, Browne K. A systematic review and meta-analysis on the effectiveness of CBT informed anger management. *Aggress Violent Behav*. 2015;25B:280–292. http://doi:10.1016/j.avb.2015.09.011.

191. Candelaria AM, Fedewa AL, Ahn S. The effects of anger management on children's social and emotional outcomes: a meta-analysis. *Sch Psychol Int*. 2012;33(6):596–614. http://doi:10.1177/0143034312454360.

192. Khoury B, Lecomte T, Fortin G, et al. Mindfulness-based therapy: a comprehensive meta-analysis. *Clin Psychol Rev*. 2013;33(6):763–71. http://doi:10.1016/j .cpr.2013.05.005.

193. Gillions A, Cheang R, Duarte R. The effect of mindfulness practice on aggression and violence levels in adults: a systematic review. *Aggress Violent Behav*. 2019;48:104–115.

194. DeSteno D, Lim D, Duong F, Condon P. Meditation inhibits aggressive responses to provocations. *Mindfulness*. 2018;9(4):1117–1122. http://doi:10.1007/s12671-017-0847-2.

195. Tao S, Li J, Zhang M, et al. The effects of mindfulness-based interventions on child and adolescent aggression: a systematic review and meta-analysis. *Mindfulness*. 2021:1–15.

196. Suárez-García Z, Álvarez-García D, García-Redondo P, Rodríguez C. The effect of a mindfulness-based intervention on attention, self-control, and aggressiveness in primary school pupils. *Int J Environ Res Public Health*. 2020;17(7):2447. http://doi:10.3390/ijerph17072447.

197. McLellan AT, Luborsky L, O'Brien CP, Woody GE, Druley KA. Is treatment for substance abuse effective?. *JAMA*. 1982;247(10):1423–1428.
198. National Institute on Alcohol Abuse and Alcoholism. Treatment for alcohol problems: finding and getting help. National Institute on Alcohol Abuse and Alcoholism; 2014. https://www.niaaa.nih.gov/publications/brochures-and-fact -sheets/treatment-alcohol-problems-finding-and-getting-help#:~:text = The%20 good%20news%20is%20that,further%20symptoms%201%20year%20later. Accessed July 26, 2022.
199. National Institute on Drug Abuse. How effective is drug addiction treatment? National Institute on Drug Abuse; 2018. https://nida.nih.gov/publications/principles -drug-addiction-treatment-research-based-guide-third-edition/frequently-asked -questions/how-effective-drug-addiction-treatment. Accessed July 26, 2022.
200. National Institute of Mental Health. Schizophrenia. National Institute of Mental Health; 2021https://www.nimh.nih.gov/health/publications/schizophrenia #:~:text = Antipsychotic%20medications%20can%20help%20make,once%20 or%20twice%20a%20month. Accessed July 26, 2022.
201. O'Farrell TJ, Fals-Stewart W, Murphy M, Murphy CM. Partner violence before and after individually based alcoholism treatment for male alcoholic patients. *J Consult Clin Psychol*. 2003;71(1):92–102. http://doi:10.1037//0022-006x.71.1.92.
202. Walton MA, Chermack ST, Shope JT, et al. Effects of a brief intervention for reducing violence and alcohol misuse among adolescents: a randomized controlled trial. *JAMA*. 2010;304(5):527–535. http://doi:10.1001/jama.2010.1066.
203. Murphy CM, Ting LA, Jordan LC, et al. A randomized clinical trial of motivational enhancement therapy for alcohol problems in partner violent men. *J Subst Abuse Treat*. 2018;89:11–19. http://doi:10.1016/j.jsat.2018.03.004.
204. Fals-Stewart W, Kashdan TB, O'Farrell TJ, Birchler GR. Behavioral couples therapy for drug-abusing patients: effects on partner violence. *J Subst Abuse Treat*. 2002;22(2):87–96. http://doi:10.1016/s0740-5472(01)00218-5.
205. Fazel S, Zetterqvist J, Larsson H, Långström N, Lichtenstein P. Antipsychotics, mood stabilisers, and risk of violent crime. *Lancet*. 2014;384(9949):1206–1214. http://doi:10.1016/S0140-6736(14)60379-2.
206. Strassnig MT, Nascimento V, Deckler E, Harvey PD. Pharmacological treatment of violence in schizophrenia. *CNS Spectr*. 2020;25(2):207–215. http://doi:10.1017 /S1092852919001226.
207. Drake RE, O'Neal EL, Wallach MA. A systematic review of psychosocial research on psychosocial interventions for people with co-occurring severe mental and substance use disorders. *J Subst Abuse Treat*. 2008;34(1):123–138. http:// doi:10.1016/j.jsat.2007.01.011.
208. Dugdale S, Elison-Davies S, Semper H, Ward J, Davies G. Are computer-based treatment programs effective at reducing symptoms of substance misuse and mental health difficulties within adults? A systematic review. *J Dual Diagn*. 2019;15(4):291–311. http://doi:10.1080/15504263.2019.1652381.

209. Lipsky S, Krupski A, Roy-Byrne P, Lucenko B, Mancuso D, Huber A. Effect of co-occurring disorders and intimate partner violence on substance abuse treatment outcomes. *J Subst Abuse Treat.* 2010;38(3):231–244. http://doi:10.1016/j.jsat.2009.12.005.

210. Substance Abuse and Mental Health Services Administration. (2019). National Survey on Drug Use and Health (Table 10.27B). https://www.samhsa.gov/data/report/2019-nsduh-detailed-tables. Accessed November 9, 2022.

211. Alsuhaibani R, Smith DC, Lowrie R, Aljhani S, Paudyal V. Scope, quality and inclusivity of international clinical guidelines on mental health and substance abuse in relation to dual diagnosis, social and community outcomes: a systematic review. *BMC Psychiatry.* 2021;21(1):209. http://doi:10.1186/s12888-021-03188-0.

212. Canady VA. SAMHSA NSDUH report finds increases in mental health, co-occurring disorders. *Mental Health Weekly.* 2020;30(36):1–3.

213. Bisson JI, Roberts NP, Andrew M, Cooper R, Lewis C. Psychological therapies for chronic post-traumatic stress disorder (PTSD) in adults. *Cochrane Database Syst Rev.* 2013;2013(12):CD003388. http://doi:10.1002/14651858.CD003388.pub4.

214. American Psychological Association. PTSD Treatments. Washington, DC: American Psychological Association; 2017. https://www.apa.org/ptsd-guideline/treatments. Accessed July 26, 2022.

215. Watkins LE, Sprang KR, Rothbaum BO. Treating PTSD: a review of evidence-based psychotherapy interventions. *Front Behav Neurosci.* 2018;12:258. http://doi:10.3389/fnbeh.2018.00258.

216. McLean CP, Levy HC, Miller ML, Tolin DF. Exposure therapy for PTSD: a meta-analysis. *Clin Psychol Rev.* 2022;91:102115. http://doi:10.1016/j.cpr.2021.102115.

217. Carpenter JK, Andrews LA, Witcraft SM, Powers MB, Smits JAJ, Hofmann SG. Cognitive behavioral therapy for anxiety and related disorders: a meta-analysis of randomized placebo-controlled trials. *Depress Anxiety.* 2018;35(6):502–514. http://doi:10.1002/da.22728.

218. Dorsey S, McLaughlin KA, Kerns SEU, et al. Evidence base update for psychosocial treatments for children and adolescents exposed to traumatic events. *J Clin Child Adolesc Psychol.* 2017;46(3):303–330. http://doi:10.1080/15374416.2016.1220309.

219. Salekin RT. Psychopathy and therapeutic pessimism. Clinical lore or clinical reality?. *Clin Psychol Rev.* 2002;22(1):79–112. http://doi:10.1016/s0272-7358(01)00083-6.

220. Gibbon S, Khalifa NR, Cheung NH, Völlm BA, McCarthy L. Psychological interventions for antisocial personality disorder. *Cochrane Database Syst Rev.* 2020 Sep 3;9(9):CD007668. doi: 10.1002/14651858.CD007668.pub3. PMID: 32880104; PMCID: PMC8094166.

221. Walters GD. Effect of a brief cognitive behavioural intervention on criminal thinking and prison misconduct in male inmates: variable-oriented and person-oriented analyses. *Crim Behav Ment Health.* 2017;27(5):457–469. http://doi:10.1002/cbm.2028.

222. Folk JB, Disabato DJ, Daylor JM, et al. Effectiveness of a self-administered intervention for criminal thinking: taking a Chance on Change. *Psychol Serv.* 2016;13(3):272–282. http://doi:10.1037/ser0000079.

223. Romero-Martínez Á, Lila M, Gracia E, Moya-Albiol L. Improving empathy with motivational strategies in batterer intervention programmes: results of a randomized controlled trial. *Br J Clin Psychol.* 2019;58(2):125–139. http://doi:10.1111/bjc.12204.

224. Van Loon A, Bailenson J, Zaki J, Bostick J, Willer R. Virtual reality perspective-taking increases cognitive empathy for specific others. *PLoS One.* 2018;13(8):e0202442. http://doi:10.1371/journal.pone.0202442.

225. Herrera F, Bailenson J, Weisz E, Ogle E, Zaki J. Building long-term empathy: a large-scale comparison of traditional and virtual reality perspective-taking. *PLoS One.* 2018;13(10):e0204494. http://doi:10.1371/journal.pone.0204494.

226. Smith S, Barajas K, Ellis B, Moore C, McCauley S, Reichow B. A meta-analytic review of randomized controlled trials of the Good Behavior Game. *Behav Modif.* 2021;45(4):641–666. http://doi:10.1177/0145445519878670.

227. Embry DD. The Good Behavior Game: a best practice candidate as a universal behavioral vaccine. *Clin Child Fam Psychol Rev.* 2002;5(4):273–297. http://doi:10.1023/a:1020977107086.

228. Flower A, McKenna JW, Bunuan RL, Muething CS, Vega R. Effects of the Good Behavior Game on challenging behaviors in school settings. *Rev Educ Res.* 2014;84(4):546–571. http://doi:10.3102/0034654314536781.

229. Schmucker M, Lösel F. Sexual offender treatment for reducing recidivism among convicted sex offenders: a systematic review and meta-analysis. *Campbell Syst Rev.* 2017;13(1):1–75. https://doi.org/10.4073/csr.2017.8.

230. Wagner DV, Borduin CM, Sawyer AM, Dopp AR. Long-term prevention of criminality in siblings of serious and violent juvenile offenders: a 25-year follow-up to a randomized clinical trial of multisystemic therapy. J Consult Clin Psychol. 2014;82(3):492-499. doi:10.1037/a0035624

231. Meloy JR, Hoffmann HJ, Hoffmann J. *International Handbook of Threat Assessment.* Oxford: Oxford University Press; 2021.

232. Fein RA, Vossekuil B, Holden GA. *Threat Assessment: An Approach to Prevent Targeted Violence.* Vol 2. Washington, DC: Department of Justice, Office of Justice Programs; 1995.

233. Cornell DG. Threat assessment as a school violence prevention strategy. *Criminol Public Policy.* 2020;19(1):235–252.

234. Reid Meloy J, Hoffmann J, Guldimann A, James D. The role of warning behaviors in threat assessment: an exploration and suggested typology. *Behav Sci Law.* 2012;30(3):256–279. http://doi:10.1002/bsl.999.

235. Kaufman EJ, Wiebe DJ, Xiong RA, Morrison CN, Seamon MJ, Delgado MK. Epidemiologic trends in fatal and nonfatal firearm injuries in the US, 2009–2017. *JAMA Intern Med.* 2021;181(2):237–244. http://doi:10.1001/jamainternmed.2020.6696.

236. Reeping PM, Cerdá M, Kalesan B, Wiebe DJ, Galea S, Branas CC. State gun laws, gun ownership, and mass shootings in the US: cross sectional time series. *BMJ.* 2019;364:l542. http://doi:10.1136/bmj.l542.

237. Schell TL, Cefalu M, Griffin BA, Smart R, Morral AR. Changes in firearm mortality following the implementation of state laws regulating firearm access and use. *Proc Natl Acad Sci USA*. 2020;117(26):14906–14910. http://doi:10.1073 /pnas.1921965117.

238. Smart R, Morral AR, Smucker S, et al. *The Science of Gun Policy: A Critical Synthesis of Research Evidence on the Effects of Gun Policies in the United States, Second Edition*. Santa Monica, CA: RAND Corporation; 2018. https://www.rand .org/pubs/research_reports/RR2088.html. Accessed July 31, 2022.

239. Wikipedia. Mass shootings in the United States: deadliest mass shootings since 1949. Accessed February 7, 2023. https://en.wikipedia.org/wiki/Mass_shootings _in_the_United_States.

240. Swanson JW, Norko MA, Lin H-J, et al. Implementation and effectiveness of Connecticut's risk-based gun removal law: does it prevent suicides? *Law Contemp Probl*. 2017;80:179.

241. Pear VA, Wintemute GJ, Jewell NP, Ahern J. Firearm violence following the implementation of California's Gun Violence Restraining Order Law. *JAMA Netw Open*. 2022;5(4):e224216. http://doi:10.1001/jamanetworkopen.2022.4216.

242. Rozel JS, Mulvey EP. The link between mental illness and firearm violence: implications for social policy and clinical practice. *Annu Rev Clin Psychol*. 2017;13:445–469. http://doi:10.1146/annurev-clinpsy-021815-093459.

243. Robeznieks A. "Enough is enough": AMA takes more steps to prevent gun violence. American Medical Association; 2022. https://www.ama-assn.org/delivering -care/public-health/enough-enough-ama-takes-more-steps-prevent-gun-violence. Accessed July 27, 2022.

244. Monuteaux MC, Azrael D, Miller M. Association of increased safe household firearm storage with firearm suicide and unintentional death among US youths. *JAMA Pediatr*. 2019;173(7):657–662. http://doi:10.1001/jamapediatrics.2019.1078.

245. Rowhani-Rahbar A, Simonetti JA, Rivara FP. Effectiveness of interventions to promote safe firearm storage. *Epidemiol Rev*. 2016;38(1):111–124. http://doi:10.1093 /epirev/mxv006.

246. Crifasi CK, Doucette ML, McGinty EE, Webster DW, Barry CL. Storage practices of US gun owners in 2016. *Am J Public Health*. 2018;108(4):532–537. http:// doi:10.2105/AJPH.2017.304262.

247. Lee E, Leets L. Persuasive storytelling by hate groups online: examining its effects on adolescents. *Am Behav Sci*. 2002;45(6):927–957.

248. A Oksanen, J Hawdon, E Holkeri, M Näsi, Räsänen P. Exposure to online hate among young social media users. *Sociol Stud Child Youth* 2014;18 (1):253–273.

249. US Department of Justice. *Hate Crimes Case Examples*. Washington, DC: US Department of Justice. https://www.justice.gov/hatecrimes/hate-crimes-case -examples. Accessed July 26, 2022.

250. US Department of Justice. Preventing Hate Crimes in Your Community. Washington, DC: US Department of Justice. https://www.justice.gov/hatecrimes /preventing-hate-crimes-your-community. Accessed July 26, 2022.

251. Stubbs J. 17 minutes of carnage: how New Zealand gunman broadcast his killings on Facebook. *Reuters*. March 15, 2019. https://www.reuters.com/article/us -newzealand-shootout-livestreaming/17-minutes-of-carnage-how-new-zealand -gunman-broadcast-his-killings-on-facebook-idUSKCN1QW294. Accessed July 26, 2022.

252. Hatzipanagos R. How online hate turns into real-life violence. *Washington Post*. November 30, 2018. https://www.washingtonpost.com/nation/2018/11/30/how -online-hate-speech-is-fueling-real-life-violence/. Accessed July 26, 2022.

253. Thompson C, Sisak MR, Tucker E. Online diary: Buffalo gunman plotted attack for months. *Associated Press*. May 16, 2022. https://apnews.com/article/buffalo -supermarket-shooting-19514b0c6524bd428f4167ad9b490a12. Accessed July 26, 2022.

254. Reid SE, Valasik M. Ctrl+ ALT-RIGHT: reinterpreting our knowledge of white supremacy groups through the lens of street gangs. *J Youth Stud*. 2018;21(10):1305–1325.

255. Blandfort P, Patton DU, Frey WR, et al. Multimodal social media analysis for gang violence prevention. *Proceedings of the International AAAI conference on web and social media*. 2019; 13, 114–124.

256. US Department of Justice. *National Gang Report 2015*. Washington, DC: US Department of Justice; 2017. https://www.ojp.gov/feature/gangs/prevalence. Accessed July 26, 2022.

257. Howell JC. Gang prevention: an overview of research and programs. Office of Justice Programs; 2010. https://www.ojp.gov/pdffiles1/ojjdp/231116.pdf. Accessed July 31, 2022.

258. Valasik M, Reid SE. Taking stock of gang violence: an overview of the literature. In: Geffner R, White JW, Hamberger LK, et al. *Handbook of Interpersonal Violence and Abuse Across the Lifespan*. New York: Springer; 2045–2065. https://doi.org/10 .1007/978-3-319-89999-2_105.

259. Christchurch shootings: Ardern vows never to say gunman's name. *BBC*. March 19, 2019. https://www.bbc.com/news/world-asia-47620630. Accessed July 26, 2022.

260. New Zealand PM says to fight hate, study social media algorithms. *Reuters*. May 14, 2021. https://www.reuters.com/world/asia-pacific/new-zealand-pm -says-fight-hate-study-social-media-algorithms-2021-05-14/. Accessed July 26, 2022.

261. Olson T. Texas school shooting: at NRA convention, Abbott says gun laws don't stop "madmen" from killing. *Fox News*. May 27, 2022. https://www.foxnews.com /politics/texas-school-shooting-at-nra-convention-abbott-says-gun-laws-dont -stop-madmen-from-killing. Accessed July 26, 2022.

262. Ramkisssoon J, Thompson K. Shooter sent Facebook messages before Texas school attack that killed 21. *KXAN-NBC*. May 25, 2022. https://www.kxan.com /news/texas/uvalde-school-shooting/abbott-political-leaders-to-hold-update-on -texas-school-shooting-wednesday/. Accessed July 26, 2022.

263. Medina D, Chapman I, Winter J, Tolan C. Uvalde gunman threatened rapes and school shootings on social media app Yubo in weeks leading up to the massacre, users say. *CNN*. May 28, 2022. https://www.cnn.com/2022/05/27/us/yubo-app -salvador-ramos-threats-invs/index.html. Accessed July 26, 2022.

264. Williams JR, Burton CW, Anderson JC, Draughon Moret JE. NIH Funding of violence research by institute, 2011 to 2020. *JAMA*. 2022;327(22):2240–2242. http:// doi:10.1001/jama.2022.5635.

265. Topazian RJ, McGinty EE, Han H, Levine AS, Anderson KE, Presskreischer R, Barry CL. US Adults' Beliefs About Harassing or Threatening Public Health Officials During the COVID-19 Pandemic. *JAMA Netw Open*. 2022 Jul 1;5(7):e2223491. doi: 10.1001/jamanetworkopen.2022.23491. PMID: 35904784; PMCID: PMC9338413.

INDEX

Page numbers in *italics* indicate Figures and Tables.

ERIC B. ELBOGEN is Professor of Psychiatry at Duke University and a psychologist at the VA. He has conducted clinical work and research at the intersection of law and mental health for 29 years and authored over 200 scientific articles. He is board certified in forensic psychology and serves on the editorial boards of scholarly journals including *Law and Human Behavior* and the *International Journal of Forensic Mental Health*.

NICO VERYKOUKIS has an AB in History from Duke University and a Master of Social Work degree from Virginia Commonwealth University. He practiced clinical social work for 29 years in community mental health centers, psychiatric hospitals, and employee assistance programs. He lives in Chapel Hill, North Carolina, with his wife and children.

www.ingramcontent.com/pod-product-compliance
Lightning Source LLC
Chambersburg PA
CBHW020253030426
42336CB00010B/750